the FLEXITARIAN COOKBOOK

the
FLEXITARIAN
COOKBOOK

ADAPTABLE RECIPES
FOR PART-TIME VEGETARIANS

Compiled by
JULIA CHARLES

RYLAND PETERS & SMALL
LONDON • NEW YORK

SENIOR DESIGNER Toni Kay

HEAD OF PRODUCTION
Patricia Harrington

ART DIRECTOR Leslie Harrington

EDITORIAL DIRECTOR Julia Charles

PUBLISHER Cindy Richards

INDEXER Hilary Bird

ILLUSTRATOR Harriet Popham

First published in 2019 by
Ryland Peters & Small
20–21 Jockey's Fields
London WC1R 4BW
and
341 E 116th St
New York NY 10029

www.rylandpeters.com

10 9 8 7 6 5 4 3 2 1

Recipe collection and flexitarian
variations devised by Julia Charles.
Original recipe text copyright ©
Chloe Coker, Ross Dobson, Amy Ruth
Finegold, Mat Follas, Liz Franklin,
Dunja Gulin, Vicky Jones, Jenny
Linford, Jane Montgomery, Louise
Pickford, Jenny Tschiesche, Leah
Vanderveldt and Belinda Williams
2019. See page 144 for full credits.

Design and photography ©
Ryland Peters & Small 2019.
Illustrations © Harriet Popham 2019.

Please note, all original recipes in this
book have been previously published
by Ryland Peters & Small.

ISBN: 978-1-78879-146-5

Printed in China

A CIP record for this book is available
from the British Library. US Library of
Congress Cataloging-in-Publication
Data has been applied for.

Notes:
• Both British (Metric) and American
(Imperial plus US cups) measurements
are included in these recipes for your
convenience, however it is important to
work with one set of measurements and not
alternate between the two within a recipe.
• All spoon measurements are level unless
otherwise specified.
• When a recipe calls for the grated zest
of citrus fruit, buy unwaxed fruit.
• Cheeses started with animal rennet are
not suitable for vegetarians so read food
labelling carefully and check that any cheese
you are using is made with a non-animal
(microbial) starter. Traditional Parmesan
is not vegetarian so where vegetarian
Parmesan is specified in these recipes we
are recommending a vegetarian hard cheese
such as Violife Prosociano or Gran Kinara,
which have the same texture as Parmesan
and are therefore suitable for grating.

CONTENTS

INTRODUCTION

Today many of us are looking to eat less dairy, meat and fish, as the host of environmental, ethical and health-related reasons for doing so stacks up. The concept of not centring every meal around an animal-based protein is well on its way to settling into mainstream society but out there, there is a whole middle-ground of home-cooks, placed somewhere between carnivore and vegan, who are doing their best to reduce meat and fish consumption, but enjoying it on occasion when the urge strikes. For these so-called flexitarians, choices are less about adopting a rigid regime, and more about an organic attempt to eat a mainly plant-based diet.

This timely cookbook is a collection of modern recipes and comfort food classics, all of which feature simple adaptations that can make them suitable for vegans, vegetarians, pescatarians and meat-eaters. So as an aspiring flexitarian, you can simply choose the dairy, meat or fish option as the mood or occasion takes you. No longer will you have to juggle between multiple cookbooks or haphazardly hash together a meaty ending to a recipe depending on your appetite or cravings!

All recipes and available variations feature symbols indicating which dietary choice they suit, as follows:

V Vegetarian – *excludes meat, fish and poultry but includes eggs and all dairy products, however cheeses should be vegetarian (see right and note on page 4).*

VE Vegan – *excludes meat, fish and poultry as Vegetarian (but also excludes eggs, all dairy products and honey.*

PE Pescatarian – *as Vegetarian but also includes fish and seafood.*

M Meat-eater – *includes meat, fish, poultry, eggs, all dairy products (including rennet-started cheeses) and honey.*

Either cook the main recipe as shown or choose one of the adaptations on offer to create the perfect dish for your dietary requirements, as well as something that you really fancy eating. Some recipes can be portioned and adjusted during cooking and finished or served to suit two different dietary requirements – a very useful feature if you are cooking for the family or a group of friends and have more than one need to cater for. Recipes to enjoy include a Borlotti Bean & Fennel Stew with the option to include pork shoulder; a delicious Mushroom & Bean Chili Sin Carne that reinvents itself with chunks of beef; Tangy Tomato Tacos with Guacamole that turn into Spicy Turkey Tacos; and a dairy-free Beetroot/beet Risotto that also works with the addition of crumbled feta and fresh mint or even smoked mackerel and horseradish cream.

Basic recipes for a Vegan Cheese, Vegan Parmesan and Vegan Cream are included (see page 8) for your convenience but shopping for dairy substitutes has never been easier (or more exciting!) so check out your local supermarket (or look online) for new products. Be aware that quite a number of traditional cheeses (including Parmesan, Pecorino, Manchego, Gruyère, Gorgonzola and Roquefort) are not suitable for vegetarians as they have been started with rennet (an enzyme of animal origin) so read the packaging carefully. Some brands now make and sell these cheese styles using vegetarian-friendly alternatives, but you will need to look for them. Dairy-free vegan cheeses (often nut-based) are now more readily available than ever before so again, look out for new products to try. Dairy-free milks and creams made from soy, rice and oats are all plentiful so try some different types and use what you most enjoy. These recipes mostly make use of beans and pulses/legumes as the protein source for a plant-based diet but on a few occasions mock meat substitutes are suggested, so again, shop around to find an (ideally) organic and additive-free brand that you enjoy – health-food stores are a good place to start.

Lastly, all of the key ingredients in the recipe adaptations (as well as the main recipes) are indexed on pages 142–143 so make use of this if you are looking specifically for a meal containing tofu, cod, prawns/shrimp, chicken, lamb or beef and so on. It's time to liberate the flexitarian cook inside you and become a kitchen alchemist with this ingenious book!

VEGAN CHEESE

400-g/14-oz can chopped
 tomatoes
300 g/2½ cups unroasted
 cashew nuts
4 teaspoons dark miso
 paste
50 g/3½ tablespoons dried
 onions
½ teaspoon salt
50 ml/3½ tablespoons
 sherry vinegar
1 teaspoon Dijon mustard
1 dash of Tabasco sauce
50 ml/3½ tablespoons
 unrefined coconut oil

MAKES 1¾ LB/28 OZ.

There are many vegan cheeses available that use nuts to provide a similar texture to dairy cheese but they can lack flavour. This is a great cheese to eat. It works well in place of cheese for cooking, or serve on its own.

Add all the ingredients, except the coconut oil, to a saucepan, set over a low heat and bring to a low simmer. Stir to combine, then leave in the fridge overnight.

Transfer the mixture to a food processor and purée until smooth. Slowly add the coconut oil, then continue to blend until the mixture is combined and smooth.

Press the mixture into a non-reactive container and chill in the fridge for at least 4 hours until firm. Substitute for dairy cheese.

VEGAN PARMESAN

150 g/1¼ cups unroasted
 cashews
¼ teaspoon garlic powder
4 tablespoons nutritional
 yeast
1 teaspoon salt

MAKES 170 G/6 OZ.

Traditional Parmesan uses animal rennet in the formation of the cheese as well as dairy milk, so this makes a good replacement.

Place all the ingredients in a small food processor and blitz until it becomes a coarse powder. Transfer to an airtight container and store in the cupboard for up to 1 week. This can be used in place of a sprinkle of Parmesan in any of the vegan or vegetarian recipes in this book that require it.

VEGAN CREAM

¼ teaspoon xanthan gum
3 teaspoons rice flour
150 g/1¼ cups unroasted
 cashew nuts, softened
 overnight in water

MAKES 150 ML/5 OZ.

This substitute for dairy cream has a good flavour. Xantham gum is available in supermarkets, usually in the gluten-free or baking section.

Pour 200 ml/¾ cup of water into a saucepan, set over a medium heat and bring to the boil. Pour into a food processor and start the motor.

Add the xanthan gum and rice flour, then slowly add the cashew nuts. Blend to a smooth cream.

Cool, then chill in the fridge for a few hours. Keep refrigerated for up to 4 days, or freeze in an ice cube tray for later use.

BREAKFAST
& BRUNCH

BREAKFAST MUFFINS

These muffins are a fantastic grab-and-go midweek breakfast and make a good substitute for jam/jelly on toast when you don't have time to sit down. They also make the kitchen smell wonderful as they bake!

200 g/1½ cups plain/
all-purpose flour
60 g/½ cup plain
wholemeal/whole-wheat
flour
2½ teaspoons baking
powder
¼ teaspoon salt
½ teaspoons ground
cinnamon
300 ml/1¼ cups plain
soy milk
130 g/½ cup brown rice
syrup
100 g/½ cup coconut oil
freshly squeezed juice and
grated zest of 1 lemon
1 small apple, peeled,
cored and diced
60 g/½ cup raisins
100 g/4 tablespoons firm
apricot jam/jelly
50 g/½ cup chopped pecans

*12-hole muffin pan, lined
with muffin cases*

MAKES 9–12

Preheat the oven to 180°C (350°F) Gas 4.

Sift together the flours, baking powder, salt and cinnamon in a bowl and mix well. In a separate bowl, mix together the milk, syrup, oil, lemon juice and zest.

Combine both bowls and mix gently with a silicone spatula. Do not overmix. Add the apples and raisins and gently mix in.

Fill the muffin cases half-full with the mixture, then put 1 full teaspoon of jam/jelly on top. Cover each one with more of the cake mixture, making sure you fill the cases only three-quarters full. If you have any cake mixture left, repeat this process in further muffin cases until you run out of mixture. Top with a sprinkle of chopped pecans for extra texture.

Bake in the preheated oven for 30 minutes or until golden. Remove from the muffin pan and allow to cool on a wire rack.

V CHEESECAKE MUFFINS Prepare the muffins as above but omit the raisins and add 1 teaspoon of full-fat cream cheese along with the jam/jelly. Bake as the main recipe. The baked muffin will break open to reveal a delicious jam/jelly rippled cream cheese filling.

GRAIN-FREE GRANOLA VE

Granola gets a bad name for being full of sugar. This tasty and nutritious granola uses natural sugars and even forgoes the grains to make it more filling. This means that you need less of it and you can layer it with yogurt and berries in glasses for a delicious and rather visually impressive breakfast.

50 g/5 tablespoons coconut oil, melted
65 g/¼ cup maple syrup
100 g/2 cups dried coconut chips or flakes
100 g/1 cup chopped nuts and/or seeds
½ teaspoon ground cinnamon
handful of dried fruit

baking sheet, lined with baking parchment

SERVES 3

Preheat the oven to 190°C (375°F) Gas 5.

Mix the melted coconut oil and maple syrup together in a small bowl.

Put the coconut chips or flakes, nuts/seeds, cinnamon and dried fruit in a large bowl and mix together. Pour the coconut oil/maple syrup mixture over the dry ingredients and mix well.

Spread the granola out over the lined baking sheet. Bake in the preheated oven for 15–20 minutes until starting to brown, stirring twice during cooking time. Keep a close eye on it, as it will burn easily. Remove from the oven and leave to cool before serving.

V YOGURT, BERRY & GRANOLA PARFAITS Add a low-fat natural/plain yogurt (such as Skyr or 0–2% Greek yogurt) and a punnet of mixed fresh berries, such as strawberries, raspberries and blueberries. Build layered parfaits in sundae glasses by spooning a tablespoon of the granola into each glass and follow with 2 tablespoons of yogurt and then 2 more of berries. Repeat and top with a sprinkle of granola and a drizzle of maple syrup or honey.

BAKED OAT MILK PORRIDGE
WITH PEARS, ALMONDS & DATE SYRUP VE

Oven-baking porridge means that you can swap standing at the hob and stirring constantly for simply mixing everything together and leaving it to morph into breakfast heaven under its own steam.

160 g/1¾ cups jumbo oats

1.2 litres/5 cups oat milk, plus extra to serve

75 g/½ cup mixed seeds

2 teaspoons vanilla bean paste

1 teaspoon ground cinnamon

3 medium ripe, but firm pears, cored and diced

80 g/⅔ cup mixed dried berries (sultanas/ golden raisins, goji berries, golden berries, cranberries, etc.)

2 tablespoons toasted flaked/slivered almonds, to serve

4–5 tablespoons date syrup, to serve

extra oat milk, to serve

SERVES 4—6

Preheat the oven to 170°C (325°F) Gas 3.

Mix the oats and oat milk together. Stir in the seeds, vanilla bean paste, ground cinnamon, diced pears and dried berries. Pour everything into a roasting pan, cover with foil and bake for 30 minutes. Remove from the oven and spoon into bowls. Scatter with the toasted almonds and drizzle with date syrup and extra oat milk as desired. Serve at once.

V BAKED MILK PORRIDGE WITH PEACHES, HAZELNUTS & HONEY
Replace the oat milk with dairy milk, the pears with peaches, the almonds with roughly chopped hazelnuts and the date syrup with runny honey in the same quantities and follow the main recipe. Serve with extra milk, if liked.

TOFU SCRAMBLE (VE)

This tasty way of using tofu looks and tastes very similar to scrambled eggs. You can use many different vegetables, herbs and spices to ring the changes and this is just one suggestion for springtime, when asparagus (wild and cultivated) is available at farmers' markets. Use a big cast-iron wok to make this dish, or you can also use a heavy-bottomed frying pan/skillet.

150 g/2 cups fresh shiitake mushrooms
4 tablespoons olive oil
120 g/1 cup onions sliced into thin half-moons
½ teaspoon sea salt
80 g/1 cup trimmed asparagus, sliced diagonally at the bottom (if using wild asparagus, then only use the soft tops)
2 tablespoons tamari
½ teaspoon ground turmeric
300 g/10 oz. fresh tofu, mashed with a fork
1 teaspoon dark sesame oil
½ teaspoon dried basil or 2 tablespoons freshly chopped fresh basil
freshly ground black pepper

SERVES 2–3

Cut the mushrooms in half lengthways, then cut into thinner wedges. Add the olive oil, onions and salt to the wok or frying pan/skillet and sauté over a medium heat briefly, stirring energetically to prevent sticking.

Add the mushrooms, asparagus, tamari and turmeric and continue stirring with two wooden spoons. When the mushrooms have soaked up a bit of tamari, turn up the heat, add the tofu and stir for another 1–2 minutes. The scramble should be uniformly yellow in colour. At this point you can add up to 4 tablespoons water to make the scramble juicy, and continue cooking for a couple more minutes. However, whether you need water or not depends on how soft your tofu was to begin with – softer types are moist and don't need any water at the end of cooking.

Mix in the dark sesame oil and basil, season with pepper and serve warm, with a nice salad and a few slices of toasted homemade bread.

(V) SUNDRIED TOMATO & GOAT'S CHEESE TOFU SCRAMBLE Omit the asparagus and mushrooms and replace with 6 sun-dried tomatoes, sliced, and 80 g/3 oz. soft goat's cheese, cut into pieces. Add these with the tamari and turmeric to the pan and finish as main recipe.

EGGS EN COCOTTE
WITH MUSHROOMS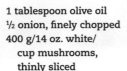

1 tablespoon olive oil
½ onion, finely chopped
400 g/14 oz. white/
    cup mushrooms,
    thinly sliced
2 tablespoons freshly
    chopped tarragon leaves,
    plus extra to garnish
4 eggs
4 tablespoons double/
    heavy cream
4 tablespoons grated
    vegetarian Parmesan
    cheese
salt and freshly ground
    black pepper

4 *ramekins*

SERVES 4

Mushrooms and eggs have a delicious affinity – their delicate flavours complementing each other, rather than overpowering, so this traditional comfort dish is given a luxurious touch by adding a layer of fried mushrooms. A hint of tarragon adds a pleasing aniseed note. Serve with toast fingers for a satisfying brunch.

Preheat the oven to 180°C (350°F) Gas 4.

Heat the olive oil in a frying pan/skillet. Fry the onion over a low heat, until softened. Add the mushrooms, increase the heat, and fry briefly until the mushrooms are softened. Mix in the tarragon, season with salt and freshly ground black pepper, and cook for a further 2 minutes.

Divide the mushroom mixture between the 4 ramekin dishes. Break an egg into the centre of each ramekin. Season the eggs with salt and freshly ground black pepper. Pour a tablespoon of double/heavy cream over each egg, then sprinkle each with vegetarian Parmesan cheese.

Bake in the preheated oven for 8–10 minutes for runny yolks, or 15–20 minutes for set yolks. Garnish with tarragon and serve warm from the oven.

M HAM, MUSHROOM & EGG RAMEKINS Omit the onions and replace with 100 g/4 oz. of finely diced uncured ham. Sauté the ham in the frying pan/skillet with the mushrooms until everything is browned. Mix in the tarragon, season with salt and pepper and divide between 4 ramekins. Finish as main recipe, using regular Parmesan if liked.

TUNISIAN BAKED EGGS

This classic North African dish (shakshuka) is now hugely popular as a brunch option in cafés but also very easy to make at home. Serve with plenty of crusty bread for mopping up the spiced tomato sauce.

450 g/1 lb. ripe tomatoes
1 tablespoon olive oil
1 onion, chopped
1 red (bell) pepper, chopped
   into strips
1 garlic clove, chopped
1 teaspoon ground cumin
½ teaspoon harissa
1 teaspoon brown sugar
4 eggs
freshly chopped coriander/
   cilantro, to garnish
salt and freshly ground
   black pepper

SERVES 4

Roughly chop the tomatoes, reserving the juices.

Heat the olive oil in a large, heavy-bottomed frying pan/skillet set over a medium heat. Add the onion, (bell) pepper and garlic and fry, stirring often, for 5 minutes, until softened.

Mix the cumin with 1 tablespoon of water in a small bowl to form a paste.

Add the harissa and cumin paste to the pan and fry, stirring, for a minute. Add the tomatoes and brown sugar, season with salt and pepper, and mix well. Bring to the boil, reduce the heat, cover and simmer for 5 minutes.

Uncover and simmer for a further 10 minutes, stirring now and then, to reduce and thicken the tomato mixture.

Break the eggs, spaced well apart, into the tomato mixture. Cover and cook over a low heat for 10 minutes until the eggs are set.

Sprinkle with coriander/cilantro and serve at once.

VE CHICKPEA & TOFU SHAKSHUKA Omit the eggs and replace with 300 g/ 2 cups cooked chickpeas and 350 g/12 oz. firm silken tofu. Carefully slice the block of tofu in half lengthways, so that you have 2 thinner blocks. Using a cookie cutter, cut out 2 rounds from each block and set aside. (Reserve the leftover tofu to use in soups or smoothies). Follow as main recipe, adding the chickpeas for the last 5 minutes of simmering just to warm them through. Next, arrange the tofu rounds on top of the mixture in the frying pan/skillet and finish as main recipe. To add flavour, dust the tofu lightly with baharat spice mix before serving.

SEEDED BAKED PANCAKE
WITH BERRIES & RAW COCOA SAUCE

PANCAKE BATTER
50 g/generous ⅓ cup
   plain/all-purpose flour
3 tablespoons coconut flour
1 teaspoon baking powder
pinch of salt
150 ml/⅔ cup milk
3 eggs, beaten
4 tablespoons runny honey
1 teaspoon pure vanilla
   extract
5 tablespoons mixed seeds,
   such as linseeds/
   flaxseeds, chia seeds,
   sunflower seeds, poppy
   seeds
2 tablespoons coconut oil

COCOA SAUCE
4 tablespoons raw cocoa
   powder
2½ tablespoons runny
   honey
2½ tablespoons coconut oil,
   melted

TO SERVE
150 g/¾ cup Greek yogurt
50 g/1¾ oz. dried berries,
   such as goji, acai,
   cranberries etc.
100 g/3½ oz. mixed fresh
   berries such as
   blueberries, raspberries,
   redcurrants etc.
icing/confectioners' sugar

*22-cm/9-inch ovenproof
frying pan/skillet*

SERVES 4

Based on the Dutch-style pancake that is baked in the oven, this is a super-easy and delicious way to make a pancake to serve straight from the pan. This recipe is packed full of nutritious seeds and served with fresh berries and a delicious cocoa sauce for a truly indulgent but power-packed breakfast.

Preheat the oven to 200°C (400°F) Gas 6.

To make the pancakes, sift the plain/all-purpose flour, coconut flour, baking powder and salt into a mixing bowl. Combine the milk, eggs, honey and vanilla in a separate bowl and beat into the flours to make a smooth batter. Fold in the mixed seeds.

Heat the coconut oil in the ovenproof frying pan/skillet until melted. Pour in the pancake batter and transfer to the oven. Bake in the preheated oven for 15 minutes until the pancake is puffed up and golden.

Meanwhile, make the cocoa sauce. Place all the ingredients with 4 tablespoons water in a saucepan and heat gently, stirring, until smooth. Keep warm.

As soon as the pancake is cooked, remove it from the oven. Spoon the yogurt into the centre and top with the dried and fresh berries. Drizzle over the cocoa sauce and serve dusted with icing/confectioners' sugar.

VE **DUTCH PANCAKE WITH BERRIES & COCOA SAUCE** Omit the Pancake Batter and replace with an unseeded vegan batter, as follows: Melt 1½ tablespoons of vegan butter substitute and pour into a food processor. Add 125 ml/½ cup almond milk, 285 g/10 oz. silken soft tofu, 90 ml/⅓ cup maple syrup, 1½ teaspoons pure vanilla extract, 60 ml/¼ cup freshly squeezed orange juice and blend on medium-high speed. Add 135 g/1 cup plain/all-purpose flour and a pinch of salt and blend again until lump-free and smooth. Let rest for 10–20 minutes before using. Heat 1½ tablespoons of vegan butter substitute in a pan and pour in the rested batter. Bake in an oven preheated to 170°C (350° F) Gas 4 for 30–35 minutes. Finish as main recipe, substituting a thick coconut yogurt for the Greek yogurt.

SNACKS & LIGHTER PLATES

CHICKPEA SOCCA PANCAKES
WITH MUSHROOMS & THYME VE

Socca are crispy-edged Mediterranean pancakes made with chickpea (gram) flour, which makes them gluten-free. They are perfect for topping with savoury or sweet ingredients. Slightly thicker than crepes, socca have a nutty-sweet flavour and a high protein content, which makes them more of a wholesome, filling meal.

125 g/1 cup chickpea (gram) flour
½ teaspoon salt
olive oil, for frying

MUSHROOMS
1 tablespoon olive oil
5 fresh thyme sprigs, leaves removed from the stems
225 g/8 oz. chestnut/ cremini mushrooms, sliced
1 garlic clove, crushed
salt and freshly ground black pepper

SERVES 2

Put the chickpea (gram) flour, salt and 295 ml/1¼ cups water into a large bowl and mix together with a whisk to make a smooth batter. Leave to stand at room temperature for at least 10 minutes.

Meanwhile, heat a thin layer of oil in a large frying pan/skillet over a high heat. Add the thyme leaves and mushrooms and cook, stirring occasionally, for 2–3 minutes until the mushrooms soften and are slightly golden. Reduce the heat to medium, then add the garlic and cook for 1 minute more. Season to taste with salt and pepper. Keep the mushrooms warm in a low oven or in a covered dish while you cook the pancakes.

Heat the olive oil in another small frying pan/skillet over a medium heat. Add approximately 60–75 ml/¼ – scant ⅓ cup of the socca batter to the warm pan. Swirl it around so that it covers the base of the pan. Fry for about 2–3 minutes, until the batter begins to form bubbles. Flip with a spatula and cook for another 1–2 minutes on the other side.

Repeat with the remaining batter to make 4 small socca.

V **SOCCA WITH SCRAMBLED EGGS & ROASTED TOMATOES** Prepare the socca as main recipe. Roast about 140 g/5 oz. of on-the-vine cherry tomatoes (on a non-stick baking sheet) in an oven preheated to 180°C (350°F) Gas 4 for about 10 minutes, until soft and releasing their juices. Meanwhile, add a knob/pat of butter to a non-stick saucepan and add 4 beaten and seasoned eggs with splash of milk. Scramble over a medium heat, stirring continuously. Spoon the eggs over the warm socca, top with a stem of tomatoes, a little freshly chopped flat-leaf parsley and a grinding of black pepper.

PE **CHICKPEA SOCCA WITH SMOKED SALMON & AVOCADO** Prepare the socca as main recipe. Top each warm pancake with slices of about 50 g/2 oz. of smoked salmon and slices of fresh avocado. Squeeze over some lemon juice, add a sprinkle of freshly snipped chives and a grinding of black pepper.

TANGY TOMATO TACOS
WITH GUACAMOLE ⓥ

There is a wonderful balance between the crunch of the tacos, spicy heat of the tomatoes and coolness of the guacamole here. Add some spiced up minced/ground turkey to turn them into a meaty-licious meal.

300 g/2 cups cherry
    tomatoes, quartered
small bunch of fresh
    coriander/cilantro,
    finely chopped
grated zest of 1 lime
2 teaspoons white wine
    vinegar
2 jalapeño chillies/chiles,
    thinly sliced
1–2 teaspoons cayenne
    pepper, to season,
    plus extra to serve
salt

GUACAMOLE
2 large avocados
freshly squeezed juice
    of 1 lime
small bunch of fresh
    coriander/cilantro,
    roughly chopped
1 garlic clove, crushed
1 red onion, finely diced

TO SERVE
8 taco shells
Vegan Cream (see page 8),
or any non-dairy cream,
    or sour cream for
    a vegetarian option

SERVES 4

To make the tomato salad, mix all the ingredients together in a large mixing bowl, adding cayenne pepper to taste; just 1 teaspoon of cayenne pepper makes a nice, moderately hot salad. Finish with a generous pinch of salt.

To make the guacamole, cut the avocados in half using a small, sharp knife. Remove the pit, scoop out the flesh and roughly chop. Mix in the lime juice immediately to stop it discolouring. Add the coriander/cilantro, garlic and onion, mix all the ingredients together and mash a little using a fork to achieve a rough texture.

Serve the salad with the guacamole at the table, with taco shells and sour cream on the side, or build the tacos by putting a large spoonful of the tomato salad in each one, then a similar amount of the guacamole on top. Finish with a dollop of vegan cream and a sprinkle of cayenne pepper.

Ⓜ SPICY TURKEY TACOS Replace the tomato salad with spicy minced/ground turkey. Heat 1 tablespoon oil in a large frying pan/skillet. Add 1 finely chopped onion and cook until softened. Add 2 crushed garlic cloves and 2 teaspoons each hot smoked paprika and ground cumin and cook for about 30 seconds. Add 450 g/1 lb. minced/ground turkey and cook for 2 minutes. Add 200 g/7 oz. passata/strained tomatoes, 2 teaspoons cider vinegar and 1 teaspoon brown sugar. Simmer for about 4 minutes, or until the turkey is cooked. Season to taste and serve on the table in place of the tomato salad, along with the taco shells, guacamole and sour cream, but omit the cayenne pepper.

SALT-BAKED BEETROOT & MANGO WITH NERIGOMA DRESSING

Salt-baking seems to intensify the sweetness of beetroot/beet. If you can manage to find different coloured beetroots/beets, it makes this an even more beautiful dish. Served here in little lettuce cups, it makes a very attractive light meal or appetizer.

800 g/4 cups coarse sea salt
3 egg whites
4 candy-striped and yellow beetroots/beets
50 ml/3½ tablespoons olive oil
freshly squeezed juice of 2 limes
1 teaspoon caster/granulated sugar
1 small red onion, sliced
1 large ripe tomato, roughly chopped
1 medium, ripe mango, peeled, pitted and diced
small handful of freshly chopped coriander/cilantro
salt and freshly ground black pepper
Little Gem lettuce
fresh mint leaves, to garnish

NERIGOMA DRESSING
4 tablespoons nerigoma
zest and juice of 1 lime
1 large garlic clove, finely grated

baking sheet, lined with baking parchment

SERVES 4

Preheat the oven to 190°C (375°F) Gas 5.

Put the salt into a large bowl and mix in the egg whites. Spread about a third of the mixture in a thin layer on the lined baking sheet. Place the beetroots/beets close together, and then pat the remaining salt mixture over the beetroots/beets to cover them. Bake for about 1 hour, until the beetroots/beets are soft when tested with the point of a knife.

Meanwhile, mix the olive oil, lime juice and sugar in a large bowl. Season with salt and pepper.

When the beetroots/beets are cooked, give the salt crusts a thwack with a rolling pin, and remove them. Once the beetroots/beets are cool enough, gently peel away the skin and cut them into dice. Drop them into the lime juice mixture whilst they are still warm, and leave to cool completely. Add the onion, tomato and mango to the bowl and stir in the chopped coriander/cilantro.

Whisk all the ingredients for the nerigoma dressing together with 3–4 tablespoons water. Carefully peel away layers of the lettuce to make cups and fill them with the beetroot/beet mixture. Garnish with mint leaves, and serve with the nerigoma dressing.

V SALT-BAKED BEETROOT, FETA & ENDIVE WITH WALNUT DRESSING
Prepare the beetroot following the main recipe. When dressing, substitute lemon juice for lime, omit the coriander/cilantro and replace the mango with 100 g/3½ oz. of cubed feta cheese. Omit the Nerigoma Dressing and instead whisk 1 tablespoon sherry vinegar, 1 teaspoon balsamic vinegar, ½ teaspoon Dijon mustard, 1 crushed garlic clove, 3 tablespoons olive oil and 1 tablespoon walnut oil until emulsified. Serve in Belgian endive cups with the walnut dressing.

PE PRAWN/SHRIMP & MANGO ICEBERG CUPS Follow the main recipe but halve the quantity of mango and replace with 100 g/3½ oz. peeled and cooked small, sweet prawns/shrimp. Serve in crunchy iceberg lettuce cups and finish with the Nerigoma Dressing.

PINK PANCAKES WITH GOAT'S CHEESE, ONION RELISH & WALNUTS

PINK PANCAKE BATTER
2 eggs
220 ml/scant 1 cup whole milk
100 g/¾ cup plus 1 tablespoon plain/all-purpose flour
pinch of salt
55 g/2 oz. cooked beetroot/beet, finely chopped
1 tablespoon olive oil, plus extra for frying

FILLING
300 g/10½ oz. frozen spinach, thawed
300 g/10½ oz. soft goat's cheese
2 tablespoons freshly chopped basil
50 g/⅓ cup chopped walnuts
6 tablespoons grated vegetarian Parmesan cheese

ONION RELISH
2 tablespoons olive oil
3 onions, thinly sliced
2 tablespoons balsamic vinegar
2 tablespoons soft brown sugar
salt and freshly ground black pepper

TO SERVE
rocket/arugula
fresh basil leaves
vegetarian Parmesan shavings

MAKES 16 PANCAKES

The beetroot/beet adds colour to these pancakes, as well as a hint of earthy flavour, and the sour-sweet onion relish lifts the whole dish.

To make the onion relish, heat the olive oil in a saucepan over a low-medium heat. Add the onions, season and cook for 20 minutes, stirring occasionally, until soft and golden. Add the vinegar and sugar and cook for a further 5–10 minutes until jammy in consistency. Leave to cool.

To make the pancakes, place the eggs, half the milk, the flour, salt and chopped beetroot/beet in a food processor and blend until smooth. Add the remaining milk and the oil and blend again. Transfer to a jug/pitcher and leave to rest for 20 minutes.

To make the filling. Squeeze the excess water from the thawed spinach and chop finely. Place in a bowl and beat in the goat's cheese, basil, walnuts and grated vegetarian Parmesan. Season to taste with salt and pepper.

Lightly stir the pancake mixture once. Heat a frying pan/skillet over a medium heat, brush with oil and swirl in about 60 ml/¼ cup of the pancake mixture, making sure it covers the base. Cook over a medium-low heat for about 1½ minutes until the base is golden. Flip the pancake over and cook for a further 1 minute until dotted brown. Remove the pancake from the pan as soon as it is ready and keep warm while you cook the remaining batter in the same way.

When you are ready to serve, spoon the goat's cheese mixture down the centre of each pancake. Top with a few rocket/arugula leaves, fresh basil leaves and a spoonful of the onion relish. Roll up and serve with extra relish and shavings of vegetarian Parmesan cheese.

VE VEGAN CREPES WITH CREAMY SPINACH & BEETROOT FILLING
Make the Onion Relish as main recipe. Replace the Pink Pancakes with a dairy-free and egg-free recipe as follows (reallocating the beetroot/beet to the filling): Combine 165 ml/¾ cup soy milk and 110 ml/⅓ cup plus 2 tablespoons water in a mixing bowl. Add ¼ teaspoon bicarbonate of soda/baking soda and ¼ teaspoon salt. Slowly add 130 g/1 cup plain/all-purpose flour, whisking vigorously with a balloon whisk. Let rest for 15 minutes. Cook the pancakes as main recipe and keep warm. When filling, replace the goat's cheese with a soft vegan cheese (such as Violife) and the Parmesan with 4 tablespoons of Vegan Parmesan (see page 8). Stir the beetroot/beet into the filling. Finish as main recipe but with a dusting of Vegan Parmesan.

CAULIFLOWER-STUFED PACOS
WITH TAHINI & LIME YOGURT

Tacos lovers, meet your new best friend the 'paco', where a palm-sized pancake provides a perfect wrap for a Moroccan-inspired filling.

PACO BATTER
225 g/1 cup ricotta cheese
3 tablespoons finely grated
  vegetarian Parmesan
  cheese
250 ml/1 cup plus
  1 tablespoon whole milk
1 tablespoon olive oil,
  plus extra for frying
2 UK large/US extra-large
  eggs, separated
150 g/1 cup plus
  2 tablespoons plain/
  all-purpose flour
1½ teaspoons baking
  powder

FILLING
350 g/4½ cups cauliflower
  florets
400-g/14-oz. can chickpeas
grated zest and freshly
  squeezed juice of 1 lime
1 teaspoon ras el hanout
1 tablespoon olive oil
½ red onion, thinly sliced
½ teaspoon white sugar
2 teaspoons white wine
  vinegar
100 g/generous ½ cup
  Greek yogurt
1 tablespoon tahini
salt and freshly ground
  black pepper
pomegranate seeds,
  to serve
handful of fresh coriander/
  cilantro leaves, to serve

*roasting pan, lined with
  baking parchment*

MAKES 6

Preheat the oven to 190°C (375°F) Gas 5.

For the filling, cut any large cauliflower florets into bite-sized pieces and place in the prepared pan. Drain and rinse the chickpeas, then shake dry and add to the pan. Combine the lime zest, ras el hanout, olive oil and a little salt and pepper in a small bowl and stir well. Add this spice paste along with 1 tablespoon of water to the cauliflower mixture and stir to coat the ingredients evenly. Roast in the preheated oven for 20 minutes until the cauliflower is tender. After this, stir in 1 tablespoon lime juice and then turn the oven to its lowest setting to keep the filling warm.

Meanwhile, mix the red onion slices with the sugar, ½ teaspoon salt and the vinegar and set aside for 20 minutes. Drain well and then set aside. Combine the yogurt with the tahini and remaining lime juice and season with salt and pepper. Set aside until needed.

To make the pacos, place the ricotta, vegetarian Parmesan, milk, oil and egg yolks in a bowl and whisk well, then gradually whisk in the flour and baking powder with some salt and pepper. In a separate bowl, whisk the egg whites until just stiff, then fold through the batter until evenly combined.

When you are ready to serve, heat a pancake pan over a medium heat and brush with oil. Pour in about 250 ml/1 cup of the batter, allowing it to spread to about 14 cm/5½ inches across. Cook for about 2 minutes until golden and then flip and cook for a further 1 minute or so until evenly golden on both sides. Remove the pancake from the pan as soon as it's ready and keep warm while you cook the remaining batter in the same way, brushing the pan with oil as needed.

To serve, combine the cauliflower mixture with the pickled red onion, pomegranate seeds and coriander/cilantro in a bowl. Divide between the pancakes and drizzle over the yogurt tahini sauce.

VE **SOCCA WITH SPICY CAULIFLOWER & CHICKPEAS** Substitute a coconut yogurt or soy cream in place of the Greek yogurt when preparing the tahini and lime dressing. Replace the pacos with Socca Pancakes (see page 28) and serve as main recipe.

MUSHROOM BURGERS v

Creamy Camembert cheese pairs well with mushrooms in this satisfying and tasty vegetarian take on a classic hamburger with all the trimmings.

2 tablespoons olive oil
1 large red onion, halved
    and thinly sliced
2 fresh thyme sprigs
¼ teaspoon white sugar
1 teaspoon balsamic
    vinegar
2 teaspoons butter
2 very large, flat
    mushrooms, stalks
    removed
salt and freshly ground
    black pepper

TO SERVE
burger buns, halved
mayonnaise
iceberg lettuce
thin slices of Camembert

SERVES 2

Heat 1 tablespoon of the olive oil in a large, heavy frying pan/skillet. Add the red onion and thyme and fry gently over a low heat for 8 minutes, stirring now and then, until softened. Add the sugar and vinegar and fry for 2 minutes more until caramelized. Set aside.

Wipe the frying pan/skillet clean. Heat the remaining 1 tablespoon olive oil and butter over a medium heat. Add the mushrooms and fry for 5 minutes, turning often, until browned on both sides. Season with salt and freshly ground black pepper.

Briefly grill/broil the burger buns, cut-side up, until just golden. Spread the bottom half with mayonnaise. Layer lettuce, a mushroom, Camembert cheese and half the caramelized onions in each bun. Serve at once.

VE MUSHROOM BURGER WITH VEGAN CHEESE & CARAMELIZED ONION
Omit the butter when frying the mushroom, using a little extra oil if necessary. Replace the mayonnaise with a ready-made vegan mayo (such as Hellmann's) and add slices of Vegan Cheese (see page 8) or your favourite store-bought vegan cheese in place of the Camembert (try Mouse's Favourite Camembert-style Cashew Cheese). Add a few slices of fresh tomato on top of the lettuce for umami and extra zing.

TENDERSTEM BROCCOLI, SHIITAKE & TOFU OMELETTE

This omelette/omelet has a distinctly Asian feel with creamy cubes of tofu replacing the more traditional cheese. This is perfect for a light, midweek supper.

1 tablespoon light olive oil

2 shallots, sliced

1 bunch of tenderstem broccoli, chopped into small pieces

200 g/7 oz. shiitake mushrooms

handful of baby spinach leaves, washed and stems removed

2 teaspoons light soy sauce or tamari, as preferred, plus extra to serve

300 g/10½ oz. firm tofu, cubed

8 eggs, lightly beaten

ground white pepper

SERVES 4

Put the oil in a large, non-stick frying pan/skillet and set over high heat. Add the shallots, broccoli and mushrooms and stir-fry for 3–4 minutes, until the mushrooms are soft and the broccoli turns a bright, emerald green. Add the spinach and cook until just wilted. Add the soy sauce and stir. Arrange the cubes of tofu over the vegetables so that they are evenly spaced. Preheat the grill/broiler to high.

Pour the beaten eggs into the pan and cook over high heat until the edges have puffed up.

Keep the omelette in the pan, place it under the preheated grill and cook until golden and firm on top.

Remove and let cool, then sprinkle with ground white pepper and drizzle with a little soy or tamari, if liked, to serve.

PE CHINESE BROCCOLI, PRAWN/SHRIMP & TOFU OMELETTE Take inspiration from the classic Chinese dish Prawns & Tofu Over Broccoli. Omit the shitake, halve the quantity of tofu and add with 100 g/3½ oz. of cooked, peeled prawns/shrimp. Add these with the tofu and finish as the main recipe. Serve drizzled with oyster sauce, if liked.

FENNEL, WATERCRESS & RED ONION GRATIN WITH THYME ⓥ

Fennel can be intense in flavour, so boil it for a while and what remains is delicious and well balanced when paired with sweet red onions and watercress.

2 fennel bulbs, thinly sliced
4 large red onions,
    thinly sliced
leaves of a bunch of
    fresh thyme
100 g/2 cups watercress
    leaves
500 ml/2 cups double/
    heavy cream
3 slices of bread
50 g/⅔ cup grated
    vegetarian Parmesan
    cheese
salt

SERVES 4

Preheat the oven to 160°C (325°F) Gas 3.

Put the fennel in a saucepan, cover with water, add a little salt and bring to a simmer over a medium heat. Continue to simmer for 10 minutes, then drain.

Add the red onions, thyme and watercress to the pan of boiled fennel and mix together. Spoon the greens into four individual ovenproof dishes, just cover with cream and a light sprinkling of salt.

Bake in the preheated oven for 20 minutes.

Put the bread, cheese and a generous pinch of salt into a food processor and blitz to a fine crumb.

Remove the dishes from the oven and sprinkle with the breadcrumbs.

Increase the oven to 180°C (350°F) Gas 4 and return the dishes to the oven for a further 10 minutes, until the tops are golden.

Serve warm from the oven, seasoned with a little salt.

VE FENNEL & TOMATO GRATIN WITH BLACK OLIVE CRUMB
Replace the thyme with a pinch of dried mixed herbs, omit the watercress and add 1 large ripe tomato to keep things moist. Slice the tomato and lay it on top of the fennel and red onion mixture in the baking dish. Replace the cream with 350 ml/1½ cups of Vegan Cream (see page 8) or any dairy-free cream. Omit the Parmesan and add 1 tablespoon of finely grated lemon zest and 5–6 pitted black olives to the breadcrumb mixture before blitzing. Season the mixture well with black pepper, sprinkle it over the gratin and drizzle the whole dish with a little olive oil before returning to the oven to finish as the main recipe.

HALLOUMI & VEGETABLE KEBABS WITH BAY LEAVES ⓥ

Pleasingly plump button mushrooms, salty halloumi cheese and juicy cherry tomatoes combine well here, offering a taste of the Mediterranean. Cook over a barbecue/outdoor grill for extra flavour but if not available, your grill/broiler will do just as well. Serve with a peppery rocket/arugula and red onion salad on the side, if liked.

250 g/9 oz. halloumi cheese, cut into 16 even-sized pieces
16 button mushrooms, stalks trimmed off
12 cherry tomatoes
2 tablespoons olive oil
1 tablespoon freshly chopped flat-leaf parsley
8 fresh bay leaves, stalks trimmed, halved
8 thin lemon slices
salt and freshly ground black pepper

DRESSING
2 tablespoons extra virgin olive oil
1 tablespoon freshly squeezed lemon juice
1 tablespoon finely chopped flat-leaf parsley leaves
small pinch of sugar
salt and freshly ground black pepper

8 metal cooking skewers

SERVES 4

Preheat the grill/broiler and line a grill/broiler pan with foil to catch any juices.

In a large bowl, toss together the halloumi cheese, button mushrooms, cherry tomatoes, olive oil and chopped parsley. Season with a little salt and freshly ground black pepper. Thread the cheese, mushrooms, cherry tomatoes, bay leaves and lemon slices onto the 8 skewers.

Grill/broil the halloumi skewers for 5 minutes, turning over halfway through, until the halloumi is golden-brown. Whisk the dressing ingredients together and drizzle over the kebabs/kabobs to serve.

PE **GREEK-STYLE SWORDFISH KEBABS** Replace the halloumi with 300 g/10 oz. of fresh swordfish steak cut into even-sized cubes. Add the finely grated zest of half a lemon to the bowl when combining the ingredients. Cook the skewers for 7–8 minutes to ensure the fish is slightly charred on the outside and cooked through. Omit the dressing and instead serve the kebabs/kabobs with store-bought or homemade tzatziki on the side.

VE **SMOKY TOFU & MUSHROOM KEBABS** Replace the halloumi with 225 g/8 oz. extra-firm smoked tofu, cut into even-sized cubes, and use as per the main recipe. Add a finely chopped fresh red chilli/chile (deseeded) to the dressing to add a little spicy heat, if liked.

SALADS
& SIDES

MELON, TOMATO & FETA SALAD

Perfect food for hot-weather dining. Sweet melon combined with juicy tomatoes and contrasted with salty feta, makes this a lovely refreshing dish. Serve with crusty bread to mop up every last drop of deliciousness.

1 cantaloupe melon, peeled, deseeded and diced
300 g/10 oz. ripe tomatoes, sliced into wedges
2 tablespoons extra virgin olive oil
1 tablespoon Sherry vinegar
2 tablespoons finely snipped fresh chives
100 g/3½ oz. feta cheese, diced
freshly ground black pepper

SERVES 4

Toss together all the melon and tomato pieces with the oil, vinegar and chives in a serving dish. Season well with pepper.

Gently mix in the diced feta cheese, being careful not to overmix and break up the cheese. Serve at once.

M **TOMATO, MELON, BLUE CHEESE & PARMA HAM SALAD** For a saltier contrast and a meat option, substitute the feta with chunks of a firm, crumbly blue cheese (such as Roquefort) and add about 100 g/3 oz. shredded Parma ham to the finished dish.

HAZELNUT, MUSHROOM & BULGUR WHEAT SALAD VE

Here raw mushrooms are combined to great effect with dry-fried hazelnuts, juicy tomatoes, bulgur wheat and a tangy pomegranate molasses dressing to make a vibrant, colourful salad, inspired by the flavours of the Middle East.

100 g/½ cup bulgur wheat
100 g/⅔ cup blanched
   hazelnuts
100 g/¾ cup cherry
   tomatoes, quartered
½ red (bell) pepper,
   deseeded and diced
1 spring onion/scallion,
   finely chopped
3 tablespoons extra virgin
   olive oil
3 tablespoons pomegranate
   molasses
50 g/1 small bunch
   fresh flat-leaf parsley,
   very finely chopped
150 g/5 oz. white/cup
   mushrooms, cleaned
   and thinly sliced
salt and freshly ground
   black pepper

SERVES 4

Soak the bulgur wheat in boiling water for 5 minutes to soften; drain.

Dry-fry the hazelnuts in a frying pan/skillet for 2–3 minutes until golden-brown, stirring often. Leave to cool and then finely chop.

In a large bowl, mix together the bulgur wheat, toasted hazelnuts, cherry tomatoes, red (bell) pepper and spring onion/scallion. Add the extra virgin olive oil and pomegranate molasses. Season well with salt and freshly ground black pepper, and mix thoroughly. Mix in the parsley, then the mushrooms. Serve at once.

V WARM HALLOUMI & BULGUR SALAD WITH POMEGRANATE SEEDS

Make the salad as main recipe, adding a handful of fresh pomegranate seeds. Slice a block of halloumi widthways into 8 slices, each about 1 cm/½ inch thick. Dust in a little seasoned plain/all-purpose flour. Heat 2 tablespoons of olive oil in a frying pan/skillet, add the cheese slices (in batches if necessary) and fry, turning once, until golden on both sides. Serve 2 slices of warm halloumi on top of each serving of the salad, drizzled with extra pomegranate molasses.

M BUTTERFLIED CHICKEN WITH BULGUR SALAD & WALNUTS

Lay 4 chicken breasts on a cutting board, place your hand on top and carefully slice through each one lengthways. Heat 1 tablespoon of vegetable oil in a frying pan/skillet over a medium heat. Season the butterflied chicken breast with salt. Place it in the pan and cook for about 3 minutes on each side until golden brown. Check the chicken is cooked through: it should be firm to the touch and hot in the middle. Rest for 2–3 minutes before serving. When making the salad substitute walnuts for the hazelnuts and fresh coriander/cilantro for the flat-leaf parsley. Serve the chicken hot, drizzled with extra pomegranate molasses.

MUSHROOM, CANNELLINI BEAN & TUNA SALAD PE

The simple flavours of tuna fish and beans are given a savoury kick by a zingy anchovy, mustard and lemon juice dressing. Serve for a light lunch or supper, with toasted rustic bread on the side.

2 anchovy fillets
1 garlic clove, peeled
    and chopped
12 g/2 sprigs of fresh
    flat-leaf parsley
6 tablespoons olive oil,
    plus extra for serving
1 teaspoon Dijon mustard
grated zest and freshly
    squeezed juice of
    1 lemon
2 x 400-g/14-oz. cans
    of cannellini beans in
    water, drained and rinsed
150 g/5 oz. white/cup
    mushrooms, thinly sliced
150 g/5 oz. canned tuna
    in olive oil, drained
1 tablespoon finely chopped
    red onion or shallot
freshly ground
    black pepper

SERVES 4

First, make a dressing by blitzing together the anchovy fillets, garlic, parsley (reserving a little to garnish), olive oil, mustard and lemon juice in a food processor until smooth.

Toss the cooked cannellini beans with the dressing and place in a serving dish.

Fold in two-thirds of the sliced mushrooms. Top with chunks of tuna and the remaining mushroom slices. Drizzle with a little olive oil, sprinkle with the reserved chopped parsley, red onion and lemon zest. Season with freshly ground black pepper and serve.

— — — — — — — — — — — — — — — —

VE SUN-DRIED TOMATO & CANNELLINI BEAN SALAD WITH CAPER & LEMON DRESSING Omit the tuna from the recipe and replace with about 100 g/3½ oz. chopped sun-dried tomatoes. Replace the anchovy fillets in the dressing with 2 tablespoons of drained capers and prepare as the main recipe. Season well and serve the salad on a bed of peppery rocket/arugula.

— — — — — — — — — — — — — — — —

SMOKED TROUT FATTOUSH
WITH SUMAC PE

Fattoush is a fresh-tasting salad from the Lebanon. Despite its exotic name, the ingredients are basically summer garden produce – cucumber, tomato, parsley and mint – with the addition of crisp pieces of toasted bread, but without these pieces of bread it just isn't fattoush!

2 pitta breads, white or
    wholemeal as preferred
125 ml/½ cup olive oil
2 smoked trout fillets
1 small head of cos/
    Romaine lettuce,
    shredded
1 large cucumber,
    cut into thin batons
4 Roma tomatoes,
    halved and sliced
1 small red onion,
    thinly sliced
large handful of freshly
    chopped flat-leaf parsley
handful of freshly chopped
    mint
3 tablespoons freshly
    squeezed lemon juice
2 teaspoons ground sumac

SERVES 4

Preheat the oven to 180°C (350°F) Gas 4.

Split the pitta breads in half and brush lightly with some of the olive oil. Put on a baking sheet and cook in the preheated oven for about 10 minutes, turning after 5 minutes, until golden. While still warm, break the bread into smaller pieces and set aside on a wire rack to cool and crisp up.

Carefully pull the skin off the trout and discard. Gently fork the flesh from the bones and flake into smaller pieces.

Put the lettuce, cucumber, tomato, onion and herbs in a large salad bowl. Add the trout and pitta bread pieces and gently toss to combine without breaking up the trout too much.

Put the remaining olive oil in a small bowl. Add the lemon juice and whisk with a fork until emulsified. Pour the dressing over the salad and sprinkle with sumac, if using. Serve immediately.

V GREEK SALAD FATTOUSH Omit the trout and add a 200 g/7 oz. cubed feta cheese and a handful of pitted oven-dried black olives.

VE FATTOUSH WITH CHICKPEAS & BEETROOT Omit the smoked trout and replace with a 400-g/14-oz. can drained and rinsed chickpeas. Add 100 g/3½ oz. of the Salt-baked Beetroot (see page 32) or diced cooked beetroot/beet, as preferred.

CHARRED CAESAR SALAD
WITH GARLIC CROUTONS ⓥ

This salad was invented by chef Caesar Cardini (of Italian descent) in Tijuana, Mexico, for American tourists. A lot of recipes for a Caesar salad add anchovies to the dressing, but this can detract from the flavours of garlic and fresh, charred lettuce that work so well together here, and leaving them out creates a vegetarian version.

200 ml/¾ cup extra virgin olive oil, plus extra to drizzle

2 garlic cloves, crushed

4 slices sourdough bread, cut into 1-cm/⅜-inch cubes

2 heads of cos/romaine lettuce, halved lengthways

freshly squeezed juice of ½ lemon

1 egg yolk

100 g/3½ oz. vegetarian Parmesan cheese

vegetarian Worcester sauce (such as Biona or Geo Organics), to drizzle (optional)

SERVES 4

Firstly, you need to make garlic oil. Heat the oil and crushed garlic cloves in a pan but do not let them burn, then leave to cool for at least an hour, while the flavours infuse.

Preheat the oven to 180°C (350°F) Gas 4.

Toss the sourdough cubes in the garlic oil until evenly coated. Spread out on a baking sheet and cook in the preheated oven for 20 minutes or until golden. Once removed from the oven, they will continue to crisp up even more as they cool.

Drizzle a little of the oil over the cut surface of the lettuce heads. Preheat a griddle/ridged grill pan over a high heat and place the lettuce cut-side down in the pan. Cook for a few minutes until just starting to blacken.

Make the salad dressing by putting the garlic oil, lemon juice and egg yolk in a screw-top jar, tightening the lid and shaking to combine.

To serve, arrange the lettuce halves, cut-side up, on plates. Finely grate half of the vegetarian Parmesan over the top – it should begin to melt. Sprinkle the croutons over the plate.

Dress the salad with the salad dressing, then drizzle with a little vegetarian Worcester sauce (if using) and shave the remaining Parmesan over the top before serving.

___ ___ ___ ___ ___ ___ ___ ___ ___ ___ ___

PE **PAN-FRIED SALMON CAESAR SALAD**   Prepare the garlic croutons and lettuce as main recipe. Allow 1 x 250-g/9-oz. boneless salmon fillet per serving. Heat 1 tablespoon of vegetable oil in a large frying pan/skillet. Season the salmon with black pepper and fry/sauté for 2–3 minutes on each side. Remove the skin from the fish and flake the fillets over the prepared salad. Drizzle with the Caesar dressing to serve (omit the Worcester sauce).

___ ___ ___ ___ ___ ___ ___ ___ ___ ___ ___

CHICKPEA & MUSHROOM FREEKEH PILAF VE

With its subtle smoky flavour, freekeh (made from young durum wheat) is a great grain to cook with. Here, it is combined with nutty chickpeas and earthy mushrooms to make an appealing, colourful Middle Eastern-style pilaf.

1 tablespoon olive oil
1 red onion, ½ chopped, ½ sliced
½ cinnamon stick
3 cardamom pods
½ tablespoon coriander seeds
250 g/1¼ cups freekeh (roasted green durum wheat), rinsed
400 ml/1⅔ cups vegetable stock
1 tablespoon olive oil
1 garlic clove, chopped
250 g/9 oz. white/cup mushrooms, sliced 1 cm/⅜ inch thick
400-g/14-oz. can of chickpeas in water, drained
salt
4 tablespoons pomegranate seeds, to garnish
freshly chopped coriander/cilantro, to garnish

SERVES 4

Heat the oil in a heavy-based saucepan. Add the chopped red onion, cinnamon stick, cardamom and coriander seeds and fry, stirring a little, over a gentle heat for 2–3 minutes.

Add the freekeh, mixing well to coat in the flavoured oil. Add the stock and season with salt. Bring to the boil. Cover, reduce the heat and simmer for 20–25 minutes over a very low heat until the stock has reduced and the freekeh grains have softened.

Heat the olive oil in a frying pan/skillet. Fry the sliced red onion and garlic over a medium heat for 2 minutes, until softened and fragrant. Add the mushrooms and fry over a high heat, stirring, until lightly browned.

Fold two-thirds of the chickpeas into the freekeh. Place the mixture in a serving dish. Top with the freshly fried mushrooms and remaining chickpeas. Sprinkle with the pomegranate seeds and coriander/cilantro to garnish. Serve at once.

M GRIDDLED LAMB CUTLETS WITH FREEKAH PILAF & YOGURT
Season 4 lamb cutlets with salt and pepper. Heat a griddle/ridged grill pan and when it is hot, cook the lamb, turning occasionally for 7–8 minutes. Remove from the pan, cover with foil and leave to rest for 2 minutes. Serve the pilaf as an accompaniment to the cutlets, with plain/natural yogurt on the side for spooning, dusted with a little smoked paprika, if liked.

TABBOULEH VE

This zingy tomato and parsley salad is a mezze classic, traditionally served as a small dish, it goes well with the Halloumi & Vegetable Kebabs on page 44.

1 tablespoon bulgur wheat
350 g/12 oz. ripe but firm
    tomatoes
100 g/1 cup fresh
    flat-leaf parsley
1 spring onion/scallion,
    finely chopped
2 tablespoons finely sliced
    mint leaves
freshly squeezed juice
    of 1 lemon
2 tablespoons extra virgin
    olive oil
salt and freshly ground
    black pepper
fresh mint sprigs,
    to garnish

SERVES 4

Soak the bulgur wheat in cold water for 15 minutes to soften.

Meanwhile, finely dice the tomatoes, discarding the white stem base. Trim off and discard the stalks of the flat-leaf parsley and finely chop the leaves. If using a food processor, take care not to over-chop the parsley as it may turn to a pulp; you want the parsley to retain its texture.

Drain the soaked bulgur wheat, squeezing it dry of excess moisture. Toss together the diced tomatoes, chopped parsley, bulgur wheat, spring onion/scallion and mint. Add the lemon juice, oil, season with salt and pepper, and toss well.

Garnish the tabbouleh with mint and serve at once.

PE MOROCCAN SEABASS WITH HERBY TABBOULEH Take 4 boneless seabass fillets. Put 4 tablespoons harissa paste, the zest and juice of 1 lemon, 1 crushed garlic clove, ½ teaspoon ground cumin, a pinch each of ground cinnamon and nutmeg and 2 tablespoons of olive oil in a bowl and mix. Rub this paste all over the fish fillets and lay them skin-side down on a large baking sheet lined with baking parchment. Bake in an oven preheated to 180°C (350°F) Gas 4 for 12–15 minutes. Meanwhile prepare the tabbouleh, replacing the mint with finely chopped fresh coriander/cilantro. Serve each fillet plated with the tabbouleh on the side.

KACHUMBER VE

Piquant green chilli/chile, fragrant cumin, tangy lemon juice and fresh mint combine to give a vibrant kick to this classic, easy-to-make, appealingly textured Indian salad. Serve it as an accompaniment to dishes such as tandoori prawns/shrimp (see below), or a pan-fried salmon fillet (see page 101).

600 g/1¼ lbs. ripe tomatoes
1 shallot
½ cucumber
2 teaspoons cumin seeds
1 green chilli/chile,
    deseeded and finely
    chopped
handful of freshly shredded
    mint leaves
freshly squeezed juice
    of ¼ lemon
salt and freshly ground
    black pepper
4 lemon wedges, to serve

SERVES 4

Begin by scalding the tomatoes. Pour boiling water over the ripe tomatoes in a heatproof bowl. Set aside for 1 minute, then drain and carefully peel off the skins using a sharp knife. Slice the tomatoes in half, scoop out and remove the pulp and slice the tomato shells.

Peel the shallot, slice lengthways and finely slice into semi-circles. Put the shallot slices in a colander and pour over freshly boiled water. Pat dry with paper towels and set aside.

Peel the cucumber, slice in half lengthways and scoop out the seeds. Finely slice and set aside.

Toast the cumin seeds in a small, dry, heavy-bottomed frying pan/skillet until fragrant. Swirl the pan regularly so that they don't burn. Remove from the pan and set aside to cool.

Toss together the chopped tomatoes, shallot, cucumber, green chilli/chile and toasted cumin seeds. Season with salt and pepper, add the mint leaves and lemon juice and toss to combine.

Serve at once with a wedge of lemon on the side of each portion.

PE TANDOORI PRAWNS/SHRIMP WITH KACHUMBER Mix 1 tablespoon tandoori curry powder, 2 tablespoons sunflower oil, 1 tablespoon natural/plain yogurt and the zest and juice of 1 lime in a large bowl. Add 170 g/6 oz. cooked king prawns/jumbo shrimp and toss to coat. Preheat the grill/broiler to high. Skewer the prawns/shrimp onto 3–4 metal skewers and cook under the grill/broiler for 2 minutes on each side, until golden. Serve with the kachumber on the side and an extra dollop of the yogurt mixed with a pinch of dried mint.

SOUPS
& STEWS

VEGETABLE MINESTRONE

2 tablespoons olive oil
1 large onion, diced
3 carrots, peeled and diced
1 celery stick/rib, sliced
1 leek, sliced
3 potatoes, peeled and diced
2 garlic cloves, crushed
400-g/14-oz. can chopped
   tomatoes
1.5 litres/6 cups vegetable
   stock
handful (about 70 g/2½ oz.)
   of broken spaghetti,
   or similar
400-g/14-oz. can cannellini
   or haricot/navy beans,
   drained
250 g/9 oz. spinach or
   other greens, chopped
1–2 courgettes/zucchini,
   diced
bunch of fresh flat-leaf
   parsley, chopped
1 teaspoon mixed
   dried herbs
paprika, to taste (optional)
salt and freshly ground
   black pepper
vegetarian Parmesan
   (optional)

SERVES 6

Having a good minestrone recipe up your sleeve can be a life saver as it's a great way to use up leftovers of vegetables that lurk in the fridge. Adapt this recipe as you see fit, and use any veggies you like to create your own favourite. For a vegan option, simply replace the vegetarian Parmesan with a sprinkle of the Vegan Parmesan on page 8.

Heat the olive oil in a large saucepan and add the onion, carrots, celery, leek and potatoes, put the lid on the pan and sweat for a few minutes over a gentle heat, until the vegetables soften without colouring. Add the garlic to the pan and continue cooking for a few minutes before adding the chopped tomatoes, stock and pasta. Bring the liquid to the boil, then reduce to a simmer and cook until the vegetables are just tender and the pasta is almost cooked. Add the beans, greens, courgettes/zucchini and parsley to the pan and continue to cook for a few minutes until the greens are tender but still green. Season to taste with salt and pepper and, if you like a little heat, stir in a little paprika.

Serve generous portions of the soup in bowls and finish with plenty of freshly grated vegetarian Parmesan.

Ⓜ CLASSIC MINESTRONE Increase the quantity of olive oil to 2 tablespoons and heat it in a large saucepan. Chop 2 rashers/slices bacon and sauté until browned, before adding the onion, carrots, celery, leek and potatoes. Finish as the main recipe, and top with a generous amount of finely grated regular Parmesan.

CREAMY CELERIAC & WHITE BEAN SOUP WITH HAZELNUTS Ⓥ

Celeriac has such a wonderful nutty sweetness. The starch from the smooth white beans gives this soup a luxurious richness, while the hazelnuts and truffle oil add extra texture and flavour. This is definitely an impressive soup for entertaining.

150 g/1 cup hazelnuts
90 ml/6 tablespoons
  olive oil
8 banana shallots,
  finely diced
2 garlic cloves,
  roughly chopped
2 celeriac/celery root,
  peeled and diced
2 celery sticks/ribs, sliced
2 bay leaves
2 litres/quarts vegetable
  stock
400-g/14-oz. can cannellini
  beans, drained
180 ml/¾ cup double/
  heavy cream
freshly squeezed lemon
  juice, to taste
sea salt and freshly ground
  black pepper
hazelnut oil or truffle oil,
  to serve (optional)

SERVES 6–8

Preheat the oven to 190°C (375°F) Gas 5.

Put the hazelnuts in a roasting pan and into the preheated oven for about 10 minutes, until they are just golden and fragrant. Tip the toasted nuts into a tea/dish towel and rub well to remove the skins, then roughly chop them.

Put the olive oil, shallots, garlic, celeriac/celery root, celery and bay leaves in a saucepan and toss over medium–high heat for a few minutes, until beginning to soften. Add the stock to the pan along with three-quarters of the toasted hazelnuts and the cannellini beans. Cover the pan and simmer gently for about 15–20 minutes, until the celeriac/celery root is very tender.

Draw the pan off the heat and remove the bay leaves.

With a stick blender, whizz the soup until very smooth, then stir in the cream and blend briefly again until well mixed. If the soup is a little thin, allow to simmer gently over a very low heat to reduce down a little – this should be a smooth, velvety soup. When you are happy with the consistency, season with salt and pepper and a squeeze of lemon juice.

Ladle the soup into bowls, scatter the remaining toasted hazelnuts over the top and drizzle with hazelnut or truffle oil to serve.

M CREAMED CELERIAC & CHICKEN SOUP Cover 2 bone-in chicken breasts (with the skin on) in 2 litres/quarts cold water. Add 2 teaspoons of vegetable bouillon powder, a pinch of dried mixed herbs and season with salt and pepper. Bring to a boil over a high heat and, once the liquid is boiling, skim the foam from the surface and reduce the heat to a simmer. Cook for about 30 minutes, until the chicken is cooked through. Strain the cooking water through a fine sieve/strainer and discard the seasonings. Use this cooking liquid in place of the vegetable stock in the main recipe. Use your fingers to shred the chicken and add this to the finished soup, reheating as necessary to warm the chicken through. Finish as the main recipe.

VELVETY PUMPKIN & RED LENTIL SOUP VE

This golden and beautifully seasoned vegan soup is the perfect comforting one-bowl meal for autumn/fall, rich with lentils and winter squash, it is very filling.

70 g/½ cup chopped leek (white part) or onion
4 tablespoons olive oil
200 g/1⅔ cups peeled and seeded pumpkin wedges cut into 3–4-cm/1¼–1½-inch chunks
120 g/1 cup carrot cut into 2.5-cm/1-inch pieces
1 teaspoon vegetable bouillon powder
¼ teaspoon ground turmeric
4 garlic cloves, crushed
2 bay leaves
3 dried tomato halves, chopped
2 tablespoons vegan white wine
150 g/¾ cup dried red lentils, washed and drained
7-cm/2¾-inch strip of kombu seaweed
squeeze of lemon juice
1 tablespoon umeboshi vinegar
salt and freshly ground black pepper

SERVES 4

In a large saucepan, sauté the leek or onion in the olive oil with a pinch of salt, uncovered, until the vegetables are soft and transparent.

Add the pumpkin and carrot and sauté until the vegetables start to 'sweat'. Add the bouillon powder, turmeric, garlic, bay leaves and tomatoes and stir. Next, pour in the wine and let the mixture boil.

Now it's time to add the lentils, kombu and 1 litre/4 cups water. Turn up the heat, cover and bring to the boil. Then, lower the heat and let simmer for about 25–30 minutes or until the lentils and vegetables are completely tender.

At this point, remove the bay leaves. Use a handheld blender to purée the soup and make it smooth and creamy.

Add lemon juice, a few grinds of black pepper and the umeboshi vinegar to taste and stir. You can add more hot water if the soup seems too thick, but it will definitely thicken as it cools.

Ladle into bowls to serve.

V **BUTTERNUT, BEETROOT/BEET & RED LENTIL SOUP** Prepare as main recipe but replace the pumpkin with butternut squash, half the olive oil with 2 tablespoons butter and omit the kombu. Add 80 g/⅔ cup of peeled and diced raw beetroot/beet with the squash and carrot, and finish as main recipe, adding a swirl of crème fraîche or sour cream.

M **CHUNKY LENTIL & HAM HOCK SOUP** Prepare as main recipe but leave the soup unblended so that it is chunky and more stew-like. Add 90 g/3 oz. ready-cooked pulled or shredded ham hock to the soup (available from larger supermarkets) before seasoning to taste. Reheat just to warm the ham through before serving.

TOFU & MUSHROOM HOTPOT VE

Mushrooms and tofu have an affinity as ingredients, and they are combined here in a fresh vegetarian take on a classic Chinese hotpot. Serve with steamed rice.

400 g/14 oz. firm tofu, well drained
8 dried shiitake mushrooms
1 tablespoon cornflour/cornstarch
2 tablespoons vegetable oil
½ onion, chopped
1 leek, finely sliced
2.5-cm/1-inch piece of root ginger, finely chopped
1 garlic clove, chopped
¼ head of Chinese leaf/napa cabbage, roughly chopped
3 tablespoons rice wine or Amontillado sherry
pinch of Chinese five spice powder
150 g/5 oz. assorted fresh mushrooms (oyster, shiitake, eryngii), large ones halved
1 tablespoon light soy sauce
pinch of sugar
1 teaspoon sesame seed oil
salt
chopped spring onion/scallion, to garnish
steamed rice, to serve

SERVES 4

Wrap the tofu in paper towels and place a weighty item (such as a heavy baking sheet) on top. Leave for at least 10 minutes to let the excess moisture drain.

Soak the dried shiitake mushrooms in 200 ml/1 scant cup of hot water for 20 minutes. Strain through a fine-mesh sieve/strainer, reserving the soaking liquid. Trim and discard the tough stalks from the shiitake and cut them in half.

Cut the tofu into cubes and roll them in the cornflour/cornstarch to coat. Heat 1 tablespoon of the oil in a frying pan/skillet. Fry the tofu for 5 minutes over a medium-high heat, turning over during frying, until lightly browned on all sides.

Heat the remaining oil in a casserole dish or Dutch oven over a medium heat. Add the onion, leek, ginger and garlic and fry, stirring, for 2 minutes. Add the Chinese leaf/napa cabbage and fry for a further 2 minutes. Mix in the rice wine or sherry and five spice powder and cook for 1 minute. Add the fried tofu, soaked shiitake and the fresh mushrooms.

Pour in the reserved shiitake soaking liquid, soy sauce and add the pinch of sugar. Bring to the boil. Cover and cook over a medium heat for 15 minutes. Uncover and cook for 10 minutes, stirring gently now and then. Season with salt. Stir in the sesame seed oil. Serve straight away, garnished with chopped spring onion/scallion.

M CHICKEN & TOFU HOTPOT WITH MUSHROOMS Reduce the quantity of tofu in the main recipe to 200 g/7 oz. Put 2 boneless and skinless chicken breasts in a saucepan and cover with cold water. Bring to a boil over a high heat and once the liquid is boiling, reduce the heat to a simmer. Cook, uncovered, for about 10–15 minutes, until the chicken is cooked through. Remove from the water with a slotted spoon, pat dry and shred. Add this shredded chicken to the hotpot 2 minutes before the end of cooking time to just to heat through.

BORLOTTI BEAN & FENNEL STEW VE

This delicious and comforting stew is inspired by the flavours of Sicily where fennel grows in abundance and is used in many traditional dishes. Serve with plenty of crusty bread to mop up the delicious red wine-infused sauce.

1 large or 2 small
  fennel bulbs
1 tablespoon olive oil
150 g/5 oz. small onion or
  large shallot, chopped
2 garlic cloves, crushed
400-g/14-oz. can chopped
  tomatoes
100 ml/⅓ cup vegan
  red wine
400-g/14-oz. can borlotti
  beans, drained and
  rinsed
1 teaspoon fennel seeds,
  crushed
2–3 fresh sage leaves
1 fresh or dried bay leaf
crusty bread, to serve

SERVES 2

Trim the fennel, making sure to keep any green feathery fronds for garnishing later. Cut it into wedges, leaving the base intact so that it holds the leaves together while they cook.

Heat the oil in a medium-sized frying pan/skillet, and gently brown the onion or shallot and fennel, then add crushed garlic cloves and cook for another 1–2 minutes.

Add the tomatoes, wine, beans, fennel seeds, sage and bay leaf. Cover the pan/skillet and cook gently for about 40 minutes.

Sprinkle with the reserved chopped fennel fronds and serve with crusty bread.

M PORK SHOULDER & BORLOTTI BEAN STEW WITH FENNEL Take 225 g/8 oz. of pork shoulder/Boston butt, cut it into 5-cm/2-inch cubes and rub these with the crushed fennel seeds before adding to the pan with the onion and fennel wedges. Fry/sauté until the meat is browned and then finish the stew as the main recipe. Check and add a little water halfway through the cooking time if necessary. Serve with mashed potatoes, if liked.

BEANS À LA BOURGUIGNONNE
WITH GARLIC & PARSLEY BUTTER

This bean-based variation of the classic French beef stew (that was once staple bistro fare) makes a filling and nourishing vegetarian dish. A garlic and parsley butter is stirred in just before serving to add a final French flourish! Simply substitute the wine for a vegan wine and a non-dairy spread for a vegan option.

1 tablespoon olive oil
10 baby onions or shallots, peeled, but left whole
2 carrots, peeled and diced
1 garlic clove, crushed
250 g/9 oz. button mushrooms, cleaned
150 ml/²/₃ cup red wine
150 ml/²/₃ cup vegetable stock
1½ x 400-g/14-oz. cans red kidney beans, drained and rinsed
1 fresh or dried bay leaf
½ celery stick/rib, trimmed
1 fresh thyme sprig or 1 teaspoon dried thyme
salt and freshly ground black pepper
sugar, to taste (optional)

GARLIC & PARSLEY BUTTER
15 g/1 tablespoon butter, softened
1 garlic clove, finely chopped
leaves from a small bunch of fresh flat-leaf parsley, very finely chopped

SERVES 4

Heat the oil in a saucepan and fry the baby onions or shallots and the carrots until they begin to brown. Stir in the crushed garlic and continue to cook for 1–2 minutes, until the garlic no longer smells raw.

Add the mushrooms and fry them until tender and lightly browned, then pour in the red wine, bring to the boil and simmer for 5 minutes.

Add the stock and the beans with enough of their cooking water to cover. Add the bay leaf, celery and thyme, pushed down well so that they are covered with liquid. Cover tightly and simmer gently for 1 hour, until the beans are thoroughly cooked and and the flavours are blended. (This can be done on the hob/stovetop, or in an oven at 150°C (300°F) Gas 2 in an ovenproof casserole dish with a tight-fitting lid.) Check the seasoning and add salt and pepper to taste, plus a pinch of sugar if necessary to counteract the acidity of the wine.

Blend the softened butter with the chopped parsley leaves and the chopped garlic, and stir into the casserole dish just before serving.

M BEAN & SMOKED BACON BOURGUIGNONNE Start the main recipe by frying/sautéing 100 g/3½ oz. smoked bacon lardons in a frying pan/skillet in 1 tablespoon of butter until brown. Remove the lardons from the pan and set aside. Prepare the dish following the main recipe and reintroduce the cooked bacon lardons to the pan with the stock and beans. Finish as main recipe.

SYRIAN AUBERGINE & CHICKPEA RAGOUT
WITH GARLIC YOGURT SAUCE

Roasted chunks of aubergine/eggplant and nutty chickpeas, bound together in a sweet tomato and onion sauce enriched with herbs and spices – this dish is popular in both Syria and Lebanon, where it is served with warm bread as part of a selection of mezze, or with rice as a main dish. Simply omit the traditional accompaniment of Garlic Yogurt Sauce or replace with a Garlicky Hummus dressing (see below) for a vegan option.

2 aubergines/eggplants
(about 500 g/1 lb in total)
4 tablespoons olive oil
1 large onion, finely sliced
4 garlic cloves, finely sliced
½ teaspoon each ground
cinnamon and freshly
grated nutmeg
generous bunch of flat-leaf
parsley, chopped
4 tomatoes, skinned
and chopped
400-g/14-oz. can chickpeas,
drained and rinsed
2 tablespoons freshly
chopped mint
salt and freshly ground
black pepper
freshly chopped coriander/
cilantro, to garnish

GARLIC YOGURT SAUCE
250 ml/1 cup Greek yogurt
1 teaspoon crushed garlic
½ teaspoon salt
1 tablespoon freshly
squeezed lemon juice

SERVES 6

Preheat the oven to 180°C (350°F) Gas 4.

Cut the aubergines/eggplants into 2-cm/¾-inch cubes, and toss in half of the olive oil, then spread out on a baking sheet and roast in the oven for about 20 minutes, turning the pieces over once halfway through cooking, until fairly soft. Set aside.

Meanwhile, in a saucepan over a gentle heat, soften the sliced onion and garlic in the remaining olive oil, adding a couple of tablespoons of water if necessary to prevent browning. This should take about 20 minutes, until the onion is golden and melting.

Add the spices and stir around for 1–2 minutes to blend the flavours, then tip in the parsley, chopped tomatoes and aubergine/eggplant, followed by the drained chickpeas. Add about 200 ml/scant 1 cup water, bring to the boil and then simmer, covered, for 20–30 minutes.

Take off the heat, stir in the fresh mint, adjust the seasoning and set aside for 1–2 hours before serving. In fact, the dish keeps perfectly well for a good 24 hours, and may even improve, and can be easily reheated.

Season with salt and pepper, sprinkle with the chopped coriander/cilantro and serve warm with a generous dollop of Garlic Yogurt Sauce.

VE AUBERGINE & CHICKPEA RAGOUT WITH GARLICKY HUMMUS Prepare the ragout as main recipe. Omit the Garlic Yogurt Sauce and serve instead with a dressing made by blending 80 g/⅓ cup prepared hummus with 2–3 chopped garlic cloves, ¼ teaspoon salt, 1 tablespoon olive oil, 1 tablespoon freshly squeezed lemon juice, ½ teaspoon ground turmeric and 60 ml/¼ Vegan Cream (see page 8) or any dairy-free cream. Drizzle over the dish to serve.

MUSHROOM & BEAN CHILI SIN CARNE ⓥ

This vegetarian take on a classic chili con carne is simple and quick to make. Delicious served with crunchy tortilla chips or used to fill baked potatoes, it can be made a day in advance and kept in the fridge until needed. Simply substitute Vegan Cheese and Vegan Cream (see page 8) when serving for a vegan option.

1 tablespoon olive oil
1 onion, chopped
1 garlic clove, chopped
1 celery stalk, chopped
½ red (bell) pepper, finely chopped
150 g/5 oz. field mushrooms (Portabellini), finely chopped
1 teaspoon ground cumin
pinch of dried oregano
½ teaspoon smoked paprika
400-g/14-oz. can chopped tomatoes
1 teaspoon chipotle paste
pinch of sugar
400-g/14-oz. can kidney beans, drained and rinsed
200 g/7 oz. button mushrooms, halved if large
salt and freshly ground black pepper
freshly chopped coriander/cilantro, to garnish

TO SERVE (OPTIONAL)
sour cream
grated Cheddar cheese
tortilla chips

SERVES 4

Heat the oil over a medium heat in a casserole dish or Dutch oven. Add the onion, garlic, celery and red (bell) pepper and fry, stirring, for 5 minutes until softened. Add the field mushrooms (Portabellini), cumin, oregano and smoked paprika and fry, stirring, for 5 minutes.

Add the chopped tomatoes, 200 ml/1 scant cup of water, chipotle paste and sugar. Season with salt and pepper and stir well. Bring to the boil, then stir in the kidney beans and button mushrooms.

Lower the heat to medium and simmer, uncovered, for 15 minutes, stirring now and then. Portion into bowls and garnish with the chopped coriander/cilantro. Serve with sour cream, grated Cheddar cheese and tortilla chips, if liked.

───────────────────────────────────

Ⓜ **CHUNKY BEEF CHILI** Omit the red (bell) peppers and both types of mushroom and replace with 400 g/14 oz. diced stewing beef. Heat an additional 2 tablespoons of vegetable oil in a large saucepan. Add the cubed beef and cook for a few minutes on each side until browned all over. Remove from the pan with a slotted spoon and set aside. Follow the main recipe, reintroducing the beef to the pan with the chopped tomatoes, water, chipotle paste and sugar but hold back the kidney beans. Bring to a simmer, then cook, covered for about 1½–2 hours until the beef is tender. Add the kidney beans, stir and warm them through before serving.

───────────────────────────────────

WINTER VEGETABLE STEW
WITH HERBED DUMPLINGS

2 tablespoons olive oil
25 g/2 tablespoons butter
3 shallots, quartered
2 potatoes, cut into chunks
1 parsnip, cut into chunks
250 g/9 oz. baby carrots,
   whole
250 g/4 cups button
   mushrooms
1 leek, sliced into rings
2 garlic cloves, crushed
4 fresh thyme sprigs
1 teaspoon Dijon mustard
2 tablespoons plain/
   all-purpose flour
1 tablespoon balsamic
   vinegar
240 ml/1 cup white wine
400-g/14-oz. can butter/
   lima beans, drained
   and rinsed
250 g/9 oz. fresh raw
   beetroot/beets, peeled
   and cut into chunks
300 ml/1¼ cups vegetable
   stock
salt and freshly ground
   black pepper

HERBED DUMPLINGS
250 g (2 cups minus
   1½ tablespoons)
   plain/all-purpose flour
2 teaspoons baking powder
125 g/1 stick plus
   1 tablespoon butter,
   chilled
handful of any fresh green
   herbs
pinch of mustard powder
salt and freshly ground
   black pepper

SERVES 4

This stew is packed with root vegetables making it both hearty enough to satisfy on a cold winter's day but still a healthy choice.

Preheat the oven to 180°C (350°F) Gas 4.

Put the oil and butter in a flameproof casserole dish set over a medium-high heat. Add the shallots and cook for 2 minutes. Add the potatoes, parsnip, carrots, mushrooms and leek and cook for 5 minutes, stirring occasionally, until the vegetables start to turn golden. Turn the heat down slightly and add the garlic and thyme. Season generously with salt and pepper, then stir in the mustard. Add the flour and stir until the vegetables are well coated and the flour has disappeared. Add the vinegar and wine and cook for 2 minutes. Add the butter/lima beans and beetroot/beets, stir gently, then add the vegetable stock.

Bring the mixture to the boil and boil for 2 minutes. Then cover with a lid and transfer to the preheated oven. Bake for 40–50 minutes.

Meanwhile, prepare the dumplings. Sift the flour and baking powder into a bowl. Chop the cold butter into small pieces, then rub it into the flour. When it resembles breadcrumbs and there are no lumps of butter, stir in the chopped herbs and season with salt and pepper. Add a couple of tablespoons of water, or just enough to bring the mixture together to form a stiff dough.

Divide the dough into walnut-sized balls. Cover with clingfilm/plastic wrap and chill in the refrigerator until the stew is cooked. When the stew is ready, put the dumplings on the top of the stew so that they are half submerged. Cover with a lid and return the stew to the oven or put the casserole on the hob/stove over a low-medium heat, and cook for 20 minutes until the dumplings have puffed up and are golden on the top.

VE HEARTY VEGETABLE STEW WITH GARLIC & HERB TOASTS Prepare the stew as main recipe, replacing the butter with olive oil and the wine with vegan wine. Omit the Herbed Dumplings. Mix 2 tablespoons of vegan spread with 1 crushed garlic clove and 1 tablespoon of freshly chopped flat-leaf parsley. Spread on slices of toasted baguette and arrange on top of the stew to serve.

M SAUSAGE & ROOT VEGETABLE CASSEROLE Omit the Herbed Dumplings and prepare the stew as main recipe. Grill/broil or pan-fry 4 good-quality plain pork sausages until cooked through. Using metal tongs to grip them, use a sharp knife to slice them on the diagonal into quill shapes and stir these into the casserole whilst still hot and serve.

PUY LENTIL & SQUASH CASSEROLE WITH QUINOA VE

An earthy combination of flavours and textures makes this a satisfying
vegan dish. Serve with nutty and nutritious quinoa for a hearty meal.

15 g/½ oz. assorted dried
    mushrooms (morels,
    porcini, girolles)
200 ml/scant 1 cup hot
    water
120 g/⅔ cup Puy/French
    green lentils
1 tablespoon olive oil
1 red onion, sliced
1 garlic clove, chopped
1 celery stick/rib,
    finely chopped
1 fresh rosemary sprig,
    leaves only
400-g/14-oz. can
    chopped tomatoes
pinch of sugar
400 g/14 oz. (1 small)
    butternut squash,
    peeled and cubed
200 g/7 oz. chestnut/
    cremini mushrooms,
    halved
salt and freshly ground
    black pepper
freshly chopped flat-leaf
    parsley, to garnish

SERVES 4

Soak the dried mushrooms in the hot water for 20 minutes. Strain,
reserving the mushrooms and 100 ml/scant ½ cup of the soaking water.

Place the lentils in a pan and cover with cold water. Bring to the boil,
then reduce the heat and simmer for 20–25 minutes until the lentils
have softened, but retain some texture; drain and set aside until needed.

Heat the olive oil in a casserole dish or Dutch oven over a medium heat.
Fry the onion, garlic, celery and rosemary for 2–3 minutes until softened
and fragrant. Add the chopped tomatoes. Season with salt, pepper and
sugar. Bring to the boil. Add the butternut squash and the reserved
soaking water from the dried mushrooms. Cover and cook over a medium
heat for 10 minutes, until the squash is tender.

Mix in the soaked mushrooms, chestnut/cremini mushrooms and
cooked lentils. Cover and cook for 5 minutes. Check the seasoning.
Garnish with parsley and serve at once.

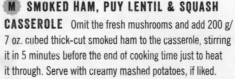

**M SMOKED HAM, PUY LENTIL & SQUASH
CASSEROLE** Omit the fresh mushrooms and add 200 g/
7 oz. cubed thick-cut smoked ham to the casserole, stirring
it in 5 minutes before the end of cooking time just to heat
it through. Serve with creamy mashed potatoes, if liked.

OVEN-BAKED GREEK BUTTER BEANS IN TOMATO SAUCE VE

250 g/1½ cups dried
   gigantes beans, or
   butter/lima beans, soaked
   in water for 24 hours
1 fresh or dried bay leaf
1 large red onion,
   thinly sliced
3 garlic cloves,
   finely chopped
3 tablespoons olive oil
1 teaspoon dried oregano
½ teaspoon ground
   cinnamon
500 g/1 lb 2 oz. vine-ripened
   tomatoes, skinned
   and chopped
2 teaspoons maple syrup
2 tablespoons tomato
   purée/paste
2 tablespoons freshly
   chopped oregano,
   flat-leaf parsley or dill,
   as preferred
salt and freshly ground
   black pepper
extra-virgin olive oil,
   to drizzle
crusty bread, to serve

SERVES 6

The beans in this dish are 'gigantes', aptly named as they are huge dried butter/lima beans that can be up to 4 cm/1½ inches long once they are soaked. Baked in the oven until meltingly soft in a rich, sweet tomato sauce, this is a Greek taverna classic.

Drain the soaked beans (see ingredients), and put in a saucepan with fresh water to cover. Bring to the boil and boil fairly vigorously for 10 minutes, then drain again. With fresh water and the bay leaf, bring back to the boil and simmer very gently for 45 minutes, until the beans are quite tender but not fully cooked. Take off the heat and leave in the liquid.

Preheat the oven to 160°C (325°F) Gas 3.

Gently sauté the onion and garlic in the olive oil in another saucepan, until they soften and smell sweet. Stir in the dried oregano, cinnamon, tomatoes, maple syrup and tomato purée/paste and simmer together for 10 minutes.

Drain the beans, retaining the cooking liquid.

Place the drained beans and tomato sauce in an ovenproof earthenware or cast-iron casserole dish, and stir well. Do not add salt at this stage. Heat the liquid in which the beans have cooked and pour enough of it over the contents of the casserole dish to barely cover the beans.

Bake the casserole, uncovered, in the oven for about 50 minutes, until the beans and the other vegetables are soft and thoroughly cooked, and the sauce is quite thick and concentrated. Check from time to time, and add a little more of the bean cooking liquid or a drizzle of olive oil if necessary to prevent everything drying out, but don't drown it. Season with salt and pepper, stir in the fresh herbs and serve with good crusty bread and extra-virgin olive oil to drizzle over the beans.

V SPICY GREEK BEANS & FETA SAGANAKI-STYLE Prepare as main recipe but substitute runny honey for the maple syrup, if liked. Transfer the beans to a shallow heatproof dish and sprinkle 200 g/7 oz. crumbled feta over the top, add a handful of deseeded and sliced red and/or green fresh chillies/chiles, a sprinkling of dried oregano and a pinch of dried chilli/hot red pepper flakes. Place under a preheated grill/broiler to just melt the cheese and soften the fresh chillies/chiles. Drizzle with extra-virgin olive oil just before serving.

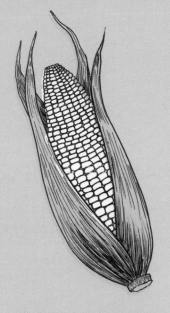

PASTA, NOODLES & RICE

SPICY CRAB SAUCE
WITH QUINOA SPAGHETTI PE

This super quick and easy recipe makes an ideal midweek supper for two people. Quinoa spaghetti is a delicious and more nutritious alternative to wheat pasta and has the additional benefit of being gluten-free.

200 g/7 oz. dried quinoa
    spaghetti
2 garlic cloves, crushed
2 tablespoons olive oil
400-g/14-oz. can chopped
    tomatoes
pinch of dried chilli/
    hot red pepper flakes
80 g/½ cup fresh white
    crab meat
salt and freshly ground
    black pepper
handful of freshly chopped
    flat-leaf parsley,
    to garnish

SERVES 2

Bring a large saucepan or pot of water to the boil over a high heat. Add the quinoa spaghetti to the pan and cook according to the packet instructions.

    While the spaghetti is cooking, fry the garlic in the olive oil in a medium–large frying pan/skillet over a medium heat until the garlic just begins to turn brown. Then add the chopped tomatoes and dried chilli/hot red pepper flakes and cook for another few minutes. Reduce the heat and add the crab meat just to warm through.

    Drain the spaghetti and put it in the same pan as the sauce. Gently mix the crab and tomato sauce with the spaghetti.

    Serve the spaghetti on plates or in large pasta bowls, adding salt and pepper to taste, and garnish with chopped flat-leaf parsley.

VE **QUINOA SPAGHETTI WITH SPICY ARTICHOKES** Substitute 100 g/3½ oz. canned (or jarred) artichoke hearts for the crab. Drain them of any liquid, cut in half lengthways and then slice finely to create strips. Use in place of the crab, reheating until warmed through.

CREAMY AVOCADO SAUCE
WITH SPELT SPAGHETTI VE

Let's be honest – any dish with avocado in it is delicious! But apart from using it for guacamole and slicing it into salads, it can also be blended with tahini to make a nutritious pasta sauce which only takes a couple of minutes to prepare.

200 g/7 oz. dried spelt
    spaghetti
1 large ripe avocado
2 tablespoons olive oil
2 tablespoons umeboshi
    vinegar or light soy sauce
2 tablespoons tahini
handful of garlic sprouts,
    or other seed sprouts
2 tablespoons toasted black
    sesame seeds, to garnish

SERVES 2

Bring a large saucepan or pot of water to the boil over a high heat. Add the spelt spaghetti and cook according to the packet instructions. Peel and stone/pit the avocado, then blend along with the olive oil and umeboshi vinegar or soy sauce in a food processor or a blender until smooth. Add a little water if it's very thick. Taste and adjust the seasoning, bearing in mind that it should be on the saltier side, since the pasta needs a strong sauce.

Drain the spaghetti and return it to the hot pan. Pour the avocado sauce over the hot pasta and mix thoroughly. Serve immediately, sprinkling each portion with half of the garlic sprouts (or other sprouts) and add a tablespoon of black sesame seeds, to garnish.

PE **AVOCADO & SMOKED SALMON PASTA SAUCE** Substitute freshly squeezed lemon juice for the umeboshi vinegar and add 1 peeled garlic clove when blending the avocado in a food processor. Add 100 g/3½ oz. smoked salmon trimmings when you combine the sauce with the hot pasta. To serve, omit the garlic sprouts and black sesame seeds and finish instead with a handful of finely chopped flat-leaf parsley and plenty of freshly ground black pepper.

MAC 'N' CHEESE
WITH MUSHROOMS & HAM

A hearty dish of macaroni cheese is a perennial favourite. Here, the creamy cheese sauce is combined with a tasty mixture of mushrooms and ham.

200 g/2 cups macaroni
   or short penne pasta
40 g/3 tablespoons butter
1 bay leaf
40 g/5 tablespoons
   plain/all-purpose flour
600 ml/2½ cups
   full fat/whole milk
125 g/1¼ cups grated
   Cheddar cheese
1 teaspoon wholegrain
   mustard
freshly grated nutmeg
1 tablespoon sunflower oil
1 leek, finely chopped
200 g/7 oz. button
   mushrooms, halved
100 g/3½ oz. pulled/
   shredded or diced
   cooked ham
2 tablespoons grated
   Parmesan cheese
25 g/⅓ cup fresh
   breadcrumbs
1 tablespoon pine nuts
   (optional)
salt and freshly ground
   black pepper

SERVES 4

Preheat the oven to 200°C (400°F) Gas 6.

Bring a large saucepan of salted water to the boil. Add the pasta and cook according to the package instructions, until slightly underdone; drain and set aside.

Melt the butter with the bay leaf in a heavy-based saucepan. Mix in the flour and cook briefly, stirring. Gradually stir in the milk, mixing well with each addition. Cook, stirring, over a medium heat until the mixture thickens. Stir in the Cheddar cheese until melted. Stir in the mustard and season with nutmeg, salt and black pepper. Turn off the heat and set aside until needed.

Heat the oil in a frying pan/skillet over a low heat. Add the leek and fry gently for 5 minutes until softened, without allowing it to brown. Add the mushrooms, increase the heat, and fry briefly, stirring, until the mushrooms are lightly browned. Season with salt and pepper.

In a large bowl, mix together the cooked macaroni pasta, the mushroom mixture and the pulled/shredded ham. Mix in the cheese sauce. Tip into the shallow baking dish. Sprinkle with the Parmesan cheese, breadcrumbs and pine nuts. Bake in the preheated oven for 30 minutes until golden brown on top. Serve hot.

PE MAC 'N' CHEESE WITH PEAS & TUNA Replace the cooked ham with a 180-g/7-oz. can of tuna in spring water (drained and flaked) and substitute 100 g/¾ cup frozen peas (or petit pois) for the mushrooms and leek. Add the tuna and peas when combining the cheese sauce with the pasta and cook as main recipe but omit the pine nuts when finishing. Finish with a handful of freshly chopped flat-leaf parsley.

V SPICY MAC 'N' CHEESE WITH SWEETCORN & PEPPERS Omit the ham and mushrooms and add 100 g/¾ cup canned sweetcorn/corn kernels, 2 jarred roasted red peppers cut into strips and 2 tablespoons finely chopped green jalapeño peppers. Add the sweetcorn and both the peppers when combining the cheese sauce with the pasta and cook as main recipe. Omit the pine nuts when finishing and dust with a little smoked paprika (optional).

GNOCCHETTI WITH SMOKEY CHORIZO & SEARED PRAWNS Ⓜ

This is a lovely summery pasta dish, perfect for enjoying al fresco – it makes the effort of setting up a table outside completely worthwhile. Its influences are part Italian and part Spanish, which can only mean one thing: it's a tasty little number, just perfect for effortless entertaining.

200 g/7 oz. large raw prawns/jumbo shrimp, peeled and deveined
1 tablespoon red wine vinegar
2 tablespoons olive oil
1 red onion, chopped
1 green (bell) pepper, deseeded and thinly sliced
100 g/3½ oz. chorizo sausage, finely chopped
½ teaspoon Spanish sweet smoked paprika (pimentón dulce)
400-g/14-oz. can chopped tomatoes
300 g/10 oz. dried gnocchetti (or other pasta shape, such as fusilli)
handful of freshly chopped flat-leaf parsley
sea salt and freshly ground black pepper
lemon wedges, to serve

SERVES 4

Put the prawns/shrimp in a non-reactive bowl with the vinegar and 1 tablespoon of the olive oil. Season with a little salt and pepper and set aside. Heat the remaining olive oil in a heavy-based saucepan set over high heat. Add the onion, green pepper and chorizo and cook for 4–5 minutes, until softened and aromatic. Add the paprika and cook for 1 minute, stirring to combine. Add the tomatoes and 125 ml/½ cup water and bring to the boil. Cook for 5 minutes, until the sauce has thickened slightly. Set aside while you cook the pasta.

Bring a large saucepan of lightly salted water to the boil. Add the pasta and cook for 12–15 minutes, until tender yet a little firm to the bite. Drain well and return to the warm pan. Add the tomato sauce and keep warm over very low heat while cooking the prawns/shrimp.

Heat a non-stick frying pan/skillet over high heat. Cook the prawns/shrimp for 2 minutes each side until pink.

Stir the prawns/shrimp through the pasta and season to taste. Spoon onto serving plates and scatter the parsley over each one. Serve with lemon wedges on the side for squeezing.

VE GNOCCHETTI WITH BUTTER BEANS & VEGGIE CHORIZO Substitute 200 g/1 cup canned butter/lima beans for the prawns/shrimp and replace the chorizo with 150 g/6 oz. of store-bought meat-free chorizo (available as chunks or slices from brands such as Cheatin') or pepperoni slices (such as Quorn). Prepare the sauce as main recipe, adding the drained and rinsed beans and chorizo for a few minutes at the end of cooking time just to warm them through. Stir into the drained pasta and serve garnished with the flat-leaf parsley.

THAI-STYLE VEGETABLES EN PAPILLOTE WITH NOODLES VE

4 carrots, finely chopped
 into matchsticks
2 shallots, finely sliced
2 pak choi/bok choy, leaves
 separated and centres
 halved
1 mooli/daikon radish,
 peeled and finely sliced
 or 14–16 red radishes,
 finely sliced
2 large red chillies/chiles,
 finely sliced on the
 diagonal
50 g/½ cup roughly
 chopped galangal or
 ginger in 2-cm/¾-inch
 pieces
2 lemon grass stalks,
 bruised and sliced into
 2-cm/¾-inch pieces
150 g/1⅓ cup trimmed and
 chopped green beans in
 2.5-cm/1-inch pieces
100 ml/⅓ cup rice wine
8 okra, trimmed and sliced
 into 5-mm/¼-inch pieces
100 g/3½ oz. shiitake
 mushrooms, stems
 removed and quartered
good splash of sesame oil
600 g/1 lb 5 oz. pre-cooked
 medium noodles
vegetable oil, for frying

TO SERVE
dark soy sauce
small bunch of fresh
 coriander/cilantro
cashew nuts, crushed

SERVES 4

This is a lovely fusion dish, taking the classic Pad Thai as its inspiration, but baked in paper to make the most of the perfumed aromas from the rice wine, aromatic lemon grass and galangal root.

Preheat the oven to 180°C (350°F) Gas 4.

To make a papillote bag, cut a rectangle of baking parchment approximately 30 x 45 cm/12 x 18 inches and a piece of foil 40 x 55 cm/16 x 22 inches. Place the baking parchment on top of the foil and fold in half. Seal the sides by folding the foil over several times, capturing the baking parchment inside, forming an envelope.

Carefully place the carrots, shallots, pak choi/bok choy, daikon radish or red radishes, chillies/chiles, galangal or ginger, lemon grass and green beans inside the envelope and add the rice wine. Seal the top and put on a baking sheet. Bake in the preheated oven for 20 minutes.

To prepare the noodles preheat a large frying pan/skillet over a high heat with just enough vegetable oil to coat the bottom. When the oil is just starting to shimmer from the heat, add the okra and mushrooms. Cook for 3 minutes, turning occasionally, until the okra is starting to turn golden. Add a good splash of sesame oil and then the noodles. Reduce the heat to low and turn the noodles in the pan to warm them through and mix with the okra and mushrooms.

To serve, place the papillote bag in a large bowl and rest for 5 minutes (don't serve the lemon grass or galangal or ginger pieces). Put the noodles in another large bowl and dress with a little soy sauce. Put the coriander/cilantro leaves and cashew nuts in smaller serving bowls. When you open the papillote bag at the table, it will fill the room with wonderful aromas.

Allow your guests to help themselves for the perfect balance.

PE AROMATIC COD EN PAPILLOTE WITH SESAME BEANS Assemble the parcels as main recipe but add a 125-g/4½-oz. skinless and boneless cod fillet to each parcel. Reduce the cooking time in the preheated oven to 12–15 minutes. Garnish the cooked fish with freshly chopped coriander/cilantro and replace the noodles with a side of steamed green beans, tossed in 2 teaspoons of sesame oil and sprinkled with toasted sesame seeds.

SOBA NOODLE BOWL WITH PAK CHOI, CASHEWS & TAMARI SAUCE

This is a great go-to Asian dish when only a bowl of noodles will do! Soba noodles are made from buckwheat flour so make a good alternative to egg noodles.

50 g/½ cup cashew nuts
340 g/12 oz. buckwheat (soba) noodles
1 onion, chopped
1 tablespoon finely chopped fresh ginger
1 tablespoon grapeseed oil
200-g/7-oz. (1 large head) pak choi/bok choy, chopped

TAMARI SAUCE
1 tablespoon soy sauce
2 teaspoons sesame oil
¼ teaspoon finely chopped ginger
2 teaspoons linseed/flaxseed oil
2 teaspoons maple syrup or agave syrup, as preferred
1 tablespoon freshly squeezed lemon juice
1 tablespoon white sesame seeds

SERVES 4

Roast the cashews by scattering them on an ungreased baking sheet and cooking in a preheated oven at 180°C (350°F) Gas 4 for 10 minutes, or until golden. Set aside until needed.

Prepare the tamari sauce in advance. Whisk all of the ingredients together in the base of a large bowl until combined.

Cook the noodles in salted water in a large saucepan or pot over a medium heat for 10–12 minutes, or according to the packet instructions.

In a large frying pan/skillet, fry the onion and ginger in the grapeseed oil until the onion is translucent. Add the chopped pak choi/bok choy, and cook until wilted.

Drain the noodles, then mix together with the fried vegetables in the reserved bowl of tamari sauce.

Toss with chopped roasted cashew nuts and serve.

_____

PE BUCKWHEAT NOODLES WITH PAN-FRIED SALMON & PAK CHOI Prepare the noodles and Tamari Sauce as main recipe but reserve a little of the sauce to dress the salmon. Take 4 x 150-g/5½-oz. boneless salmon fillets and season with salt and black pepper. Heat 2 tablespoons of oil in a large frying pan/skillet and fry the salmon skin-side down for 2–3 minutes, then turn over and fry for a further 1–2 minutes, or until cooked through. Place the salmon skin-side up on top of a bowl of the warm noodles and spoon the reserved dressing over each serving.

_____

BEETROOT RISOTTO ⑳

A risotto is a great staple for everyday eating. This simple vegan recipe
is particularly tasty and its colour will always be a conversation point too.

500 g/1 lb 2 oz. raw
    beetroot/beets
    (about 2 medium–large)
2 teaspoons olive oil
2 red onions, finely chopped
2 garlic cloves, crushed
6–8-cm/2½–3-inch piece
    of fresh ginger, peeled
    and grated
400 g/generous 2 cups
    risotto rice, such as
    Arborio
200 ml/1 scant cup vegan
    white wine
850 ml/3½ cups vegetable
    stock
grated zest and freshly
    squeezed juice of
    1–2 lemons, to taste
3 fresh thyme sprigs,
    leaves finely chopped
salt and freshly ground
    black pepper
freshly chopped flat-leaf
    parsley, to serve

SERVES 4

Preheat the oven to 200°C (400°F) Gas 6.

Individually wrap the beetroot/beets in kitchen foil and put them
on a baking sheet. Bake in the preheated oven for about 40 minutes,
or until tender. Set aside until cool enough to handle, then rub off
the skin using the foil and cut the beetroot/beets into cubes. Set aside.

Heat the olive oil in a heavy-based saucepan, add the onions and
cook over a low heat for about 10 minutes until soft but not coloured.
Add 2 tablespoons of water to the pan if the onions are sticking. Stir
in the garlic and ginger and cook for 1–2 minutes. Add the rice and
cook until it turns opaque. Add the wine and stir until absorbed. Add
a quarter of the stock and stir until all the liquid has been absorbed.

Continue to add the stock in stages, stirring constantly until the rice
is soft but still has bite. Remove from the heat, then stir in the lemon
zest and juice. Next stir in the beetroot/beet and thyme, and season
with salt and pepper. The consistency should be thick and creamy;
add additional stock if required.

Spoon into warmed serving bowls and sprinkle with the chopped
parsley. Serve immediately.

Ⓥ BEETROOT & FETA RISOTTO WITH MINT Prepare the risotto as main recipe.
Add 100 g/3½ oz. crumbled feta to the warm risotto and stir in until molten. Omit the fresh
thyme and parsley and add some freshly chopped mint leaves as a garnish just before serving.

**ⓅⒺ BEETROOT & SMOKED MACKEREL RISOTTO WITH HORSERADISH
CREAM** Prepare the risotto as main recipe. Take 140 g/5 oz. boneless hot smoked mackerel
fillets. Remove the skin, break the fish into chunky pieces and fold these into the cooked risotto.
Spoon into serving bowls. Mix 1 tablespoon of horseradish sauce with 3 tablespoons of crème
fraîche or sour cream and swirl a spoonful of this mixture into each serving.

SPICED ALMOND PILAF VE

Delicately flavoured with fragrant spices, this nutty basmati rice dish is delicious on its own as a light vegan main, or served as an accompaniment to other dishes.

1½ tablespoons vegetable oil
1 shallot, finely chopped
1 cinnamon stick
2 cardamom pods
200 g/1 cup basmati rice, rinsed
1 tablespoon tomato purée/paste
225 g/8 oz. ripe tomatoes
25 g/3 tablespoons flaked/slivered almonds, dry-fried until golden
freshly chopped coriander/cilantro, to garnish
salt

SERVES 4

Heat the oil in a heavy-bottomed saucepan set over a medium heat. Add the shallot, cinnamon stick and cardamom pods and fry gently, stirring now and then, for 2 minutes, until the shallot softens.

Mix in the basmati rice, coating well with the oil, then the tomato purée/paste. Pour over 300 ml/1¼ cups of water and season with salt. Bring the mixture to the boil, reduce the heat, cover and simmer for 10–15 minutes, until the water has all been absorbed and the rice is tender.

Meanwhile, scald the tomatoes. Pour boiling water over the tomatoes in a small pan or pot set over a medium heat. Heat for 1 minute, then remove from the water and carefully peel off the skin using a sharp knife. Halve the tomatoes, scoop out the soft pulp and finely dice the tomato shells.

When the rice is cooked, transfer to a serving dish. Fold in the diced tomatoes, sprinkle with the flaked/slivered almonds and coriander/cilantro, and serve at once.

M ROAST LEMON & SUMAC CHICKEN WITH TOMATO PILAF Take 6–8 chicken thighs, rinse and pat dry with paper towels. Preheat the oven to 180°C (350°F) Gas 4. Put the freshly squeezed juice of half a lemon, 1 tablespoon of sumac, 4 crushed garlic cloves, 1 teaspoon salt and 2 tablespoons olive oil in a large bowl. Add the chicken thighs and toss to cover in the marinade. Slice an unwaxed lemon and lay it in a baking dish. Lay the chicken skin-side up over the top. Roast, uncovered, in the preheated oven for about 30–40 minutes, until cooked. The juice should run clear when you pierce a thigh. Serve hot with the pilaf on the side.

CATALAN RICE WITH SMOKED HADDOCK & ROASTED PEPPERS PE

Based on a traditional Spanish recipe, this rice dish gets both its unique flavour and colour from saffron. Simply omit the fish for a tasty vegetarian option.

300 g/10 oz. undyed
    smoked haddock fillet
400-g/14-oz. can chickpeas,
    drained and rinsed
generous pinch of saffron
    strands
1 red (bell) pepper, halved
    lengthways and deseeded
2 large tomatoes
3 tablespoons olive oil
6 garlic cloves, finely
    chopped
250 g/1¼ cups short-grain
    rice, such as Bomba
    or Arborio
2 hard-boiled/hard-cooked
    eggs, peeled and cut
    into quarters

SERVES 4

Poach the smoked haddock gently in water for 5 minutes and drain. Flake the fish with a fork, removing any stray bones, and set aside.

Warm the chickpeas in a little water, crumbling the strands of saffron into the pan. Simmer very gently for about 20 minutes so that they take on the colour and flavour of the saffron. Drain through a sieve/strainer, reserving the saffron-infused cooking water, and set both aside.

Put the red (bell) pepper halves under a preheated grill/broiler, skin-side up, until the skins blacken. Transfer to a plastic bag for a few minutes, then lift off the blackened skins and slice the flesh into strips.

Blanch the tomatoes in boiling water for 1 minute, peel, deseed and chop the flesh.

Heat the olive oil in a large saucepan and cook the garlic gently for 1–2 minutes, until it becomes golden, being careful not to burn it. Add the tomato pulp and cook for another 5 minutes or so, until it has disintegrated, and then tip the rice into the pan and stir thoroughly until every grain is coated. Add 600 ml/2½ cups of water (including the reserved saffron-infused water) and bring to the boil. Simmer for 20 minutes, uncovered, until the rice is cooked and no liquid remains.

Stir in the chickpeas and flaked fish, heat through for a few minutes, then strew the strips of red (bell) pepper over. Place the hard-boiled/hard-cooked egg quarters on top and serve.

VE SPANISH-STYLE SAFFRON RICE WITH PAPRIKA HEARTS OF PALM

Prepare the rice as main recipe omitting the smoked haddock and eggs and keep warm until ready to serve. Take a 400-g/14-oz. can of hearts of palm. Drain and slice into 1.5-cm/½-inch slices. Lay these on paper towels to absorb their moisture and sprinkle with ½ teaspoon of Spanish smoked paprika and season with salt and pepper. Heat 1 tablespoon of vegetable oil over a medium-high heat until very hot. Add to the hot pan, seasoned-side down, and sprinkle with another ½ teaspoon of smoked paprika and season again. Cook for 1–2 minutes on each side, or until starting to brown. Remove from the heat and arrange on top of each serving of rice. Serve with a simple aioli made by blending a crushed garlic clove with 4 tablespoons of store-bought vegan mayonnaise and add a spoonful to the top of each serving (optional).

VEGETABLE JAMBALAYA ⓥ

Jambalaya may have its origins in Spanish paella, but here, it has added heat with chilli/chile and smokey flavour with paprika. Roasting the okra and broccoli gives it a wonderful nutty flavour and a crisp texture.

1 green (bell) pepper, deseeded and finely diced
1 red (bell) pepper, deseeded and finely diced
4 sticks/ribs celery, thinly sliced
2 onions, finely diced
2 teaspoons smoked Spanish paprika
2 fresh red chillies/chiles, thinly sliced
500 g/2½ cups short-grain rice, such as Bomba or Arborio
1 litre/quart vegetable stock
100 g/½ cup frozen peas
50 g/⅓ cup frozen sweetcorn kernels
100 g/3½ oz. fresh okra, trimmed and halved lengthways
100 g/3½ oz. broccoli florets
100 g/1 heaped cup mangetout/snow peas or sugarsnap beans, trimmed
4 tomatoes, quartered
salt
vegetable oil, for frying and roasting

SERVES 4

Preheat the oven to 180°C (350°F) Gas 4.

In a large saucepan, cover the base with vegetable oil and bring to a moderate temperature over a medium heat. Add the (bell) peppers, celery, onions and smoked paprika and allow them to cook for a few minutes, stirring regularly, until the vegetables are starting to turn golden and catch on the base of the pan. Add the chillies/chiles, then the rice and stir to just coat the rice with the oil. Now add the stock and a level teaspoon of table salt and bring to a low simmer. Continue to simmer for 10 minutes.

Add the frozen peas and sweetcorn, and bring back to a simmer. Continue to simmer for another 5 minutes, until the rice is cooked.

While the rice is cooking, put the okra and broccoli on a baking sheet, drizzle with oil and add a good sprinkle of salt. Toss to coat evenly, then roast them in the preheated oven for 10 minutes.

Once the rice is cooked, add the mangetout/snow peas or sugarsnap beans and tomatoes, and stir through.

Serve the rice onto warm plates and place the roasted okra and broccoli on top to finish the jambalaya.

PE JAMBALAYA WITH PAN-FRIED GARLIC PRAWNS Prepare the jambalaya as main recipe but omit the fresh chilli/chile. Keep warm until ready to serve. Gently melt 25 g/2 tablespoons butter with 2 tablespoons olive oil in a frying pan/skillet. Add 3 cloves of chopped garlic, 1 finely chopped fresh red chilli/chile (leaving the seeds in for extra heat). Fry for 1–2 minutes until the garlic is just turning brown. Turn up the heat, add 12–20 shell-on raw king prawns/jumbo shrimp to the pan and fry until they turn pink. Remove from the heat, season with salt and pepper and stir in the freshly squeezed juice of 1 lemon plus a handful of freshly chopped flat-leaf parsley. Divide the hot prawns/shrimp between each serving.

ASPARAGUS RISOTTO ⓥ

4 carrots, peeled
2 celery sticks/ribs
3 onions
400 g/14 oz. fresh asparagus
80 g/1¼ cups baby spinach
   leaves, washed
2 garlic cloves, finely sliced
350 g/2 cups Arborio rice
200 ml/1 scant cup white
   wine
80 g/1¼ cup grated
   vegetarian Parmesan
   cheese
grated zest of ½ lemon
a knob/pat of butter
salt
olive oil, for frying

SERVES 4

This creamy and rich recipe is a great way to enjoy the flavour of asparagus, and the dramatic appearance of a vibrant green risotto makes it great fun, too.

To make an asparagus stock, finely dice the carrots, celery and 2 of the onions and put in a large saucepan with 1 litre/quart of water.

Trim about 2.5 cm/1 inch from the base of the asparagus spears and discard. Trim a further 2.5 cm/1 inch from the base of the spears, finely slice them and place in the stock water. Bring the stock to a low simmer and cook for 45 minutes. Add the spinach and simmer for 2 minutes, then blend the stock with a handheld electric blender until smooth.

Add a little oil to a large heavy-based non-stick saucepan. Finely dice the remaining onion and add to the pan with the garlic and cook over a very low heat until just translucent. Add the rice and cook, gently stirring, until the rice is covered with oil and starts to go opaque. Add the wine and simmer until the wine is nearly all absorbed. Stirring constantly, add half of the asparagus stock and a pinch of salt and continue cooking on a low simmer until all of the stock is absorbed. Continue adding the remaining stock a little at a time until the rice is cooked and has just a little bite when tasted (there should be no excess liquid).

To finish, beat in the Parmesan cheese, lemon zest and a knob/pat of butter to loosen the risotto. Add the asparagus and serve.

VE ASPARAGUS & PEA RISOTTO Prepare as main recipe, adding a handful of frozen petit pois with the last ladle of asparagus stock. Replace the wine with vegan wine, omit the vegetarian Parmesan and use a little olive oil to loosen the risotto in place of the butter. Finish each serving with a sprinkle of Vegan Parmesan (see page 8).

M ASPARAGUS RISOTTO WITH PROSCIUTTO Prepare as main recipe. Cut 3 slices of Prosciutto into strips and stir them into the rice along with the asparagus tips.

OVEN BAKES
& SHEET PANS

BUTTERNUT & CAULIFLOWER LENTIL KORMA VE

This is a very cost-effective and colourful vegan tray bake, combining sweet but not too starchy butternut squash and cauliflower with lentils and spices and coconut milk. It is a mild curry that will tempt reluctant vegans!

2 red onions, cut into quarters

400 g/14 oz. butternut squash, peeled, deseeded and cut into 1-cm/½-inch cubes

½ cauliflower, cut into florets

2 teaspoons olive oil

60 g/¼ cup korma curry paste

200 ml/scant 1 cup coconut milk

400-g/14-oz. can green lentils, drained and rinsed

1 lemon, cut into quarters, to serve

1 tablespoon freshly chopped coriander/ cilantro, to serve

SERVES 2

Preheat the oven to 200°C (400°F) Gas 6.

Put the onions, butternut squash and cauliflower in a sheet pan with sides and drizzle over the olive oil.

Bake in the preheated oven for 30–35 minutes until all the vegetables are soft and the cauliflower is also brown and crispy at the edges.

Meanwhile, mix the curry paste and coconut milk together. Pour the mixture over the vegetables and stir in the lentils.

Bake for a further 10 minutes. Squeeze over the lemon quarters, sprinkle over the coriander/cilantro and serve.

V CURRIED VEGETABLE SHEET PAN WITH PANEER & NIGELLA SEEDS

Add 225 g/8 oz. paneer (Indian firm cheese), cut into 2-cm/¾-inch cubes. Toss the cubes with the vegetables and cook as main recipe. Add a sprinkling of nigella seeds after you add the curry paste mixture and before returning to the oven.

STUFFED MUSHROOMS

A perfect example of no-waste cooking, this recipe makes use of the stalks of the mushrooms to stuff the caps, along with breadcrumbs and fragrant basil pesto.

4 large, even-sized field/
    meadow mushrooms,
    each approx. 9-cm/
    3½-inch diameter
100 g/1⅓ cups fresh
    breadcrumbs
3 tablespoons store-bought
    fresh basil pesto
3 tablespoons olive oil
25 g/⅓ cup grated
    vegetarian Parmesan
    cheese
2 tablespoons pine nuts
salt and freshly ground
    black pepper

SERVES 4

Preheat the oven to 200°C (400°F) Gas 6.

Trim the stalks off the mushrooms and finely chop. Mix together the chopped stalks, breadcrumbs, pesto, 2 tablespoons olive oil, Parmesan cheese and pine nuts.

Brush the skin side of the mushroom caps lightly with olive oil. Place skin-side down on a baking sheet. Season the inside of the mushroom caps with salt and pepper. Fill each mushroom cap with the pesto mixture, pressing it in firmly. Drizzle the surface of the filled mushrooms with the remaining olive oil.

Bake in the preheated oven for 20 minutes and serve at once.

VE SAGE & WALNUT PESTO MUSHROOMS WITH CRANBERRIES Blend 15 g/1 cup fresh sage, 15 g/1 cup fresh flat-leaf parsley, 3 cloves garlic and 130 g/1 cup toasted walnuts in a food processor for 15 seconds. Add 2 tablespoons freshly squeezed lemon juice and pour 125 ml/½ cup olive oil through the pour spout at the top. Finish by blending in up to 65 ml/¼ cup water to achieve the desired consistency. Prepare and cook as main recipe, adding 2 tablespoons of dried cranberries to the mushroom mixture in the frying pan/skillet and substituting the sage and walnut pesto for the basil pesto. Add a sprinkling of chopped walnuts to each filled mushroom before baking.

CHEESY LENTIL BAKE

This thrifty and humble recipe dates from the Second World War, when rationing was in force and meat was scarce. It will emerge from the oven with a deliciously crisp and golden top. Serve with a side of broccoli or green beans, if liked.

300 g/1½ cups dried
    red lentils
30 g/2 tablespoons butter
1 onion, chopped
900 ml/3¾ cups milk
125 g/4 oz. Cheddar cheese,
    grated
2 tablespoons fresh
    breadcrumbs
salt and freshly ground
    black pepper

*a 1-litre/quart capacity
gratin dish, well buttered*

SERVES 4

Rinse the lentils and soak in cold water for 1 hour, then drain. Melt the butter in a medium-sized saucepan, and fry the onion very gently until soft and beginning to brown. This will take about 15 minutes.

Next, pour the milk into the pan and add the drained lentils, then stir around and bring to the boil. Once it has boiled, turn down the heat and simmer, uncovered, until the lentils are soft, which will take about an hour. Stir the mixture from time to time to prevent it sticking to the bottom of the pan, and if the liquid seems to be evaporating too fast, half-cover the pan, or top up with a little hot water, but don't let the mixture become too sloppy. It should be the texture of loose porridge/oatmeal when it is cooked.

Preheat the oven to 180°C (350°F) Gas 4.

When the lentils are cooked, season to taste with a little salt – don't overdo the salt as the cheese is salty – and pepper. Stir in half of the grated cheese.

Spoon the lentil and cheese mixture into the prepared gratin dish. Mix together the breadcrumbs and remaining cheese, then sprinkle over the top. Bake in the preheated oven for about 20–30 minutes, until the top is nicely crisp and golden. Serve immediately.

——— ——— ——— ——— ——— ——— ——— ——— ——— ——— ———

M CHEESE & BACON LENTILS WITH POACHED EGGS Roughly chop 4 rashers/slices streaky bacon and add to the frying pan/skillet with the onion and cook as main recipe. Top each serving with a poached egg and a few dashes of a hot sauce, such as Tabasco, if liked.

——— ——— ——— ——— ——— ——— ——— ——— ——— ——— ———

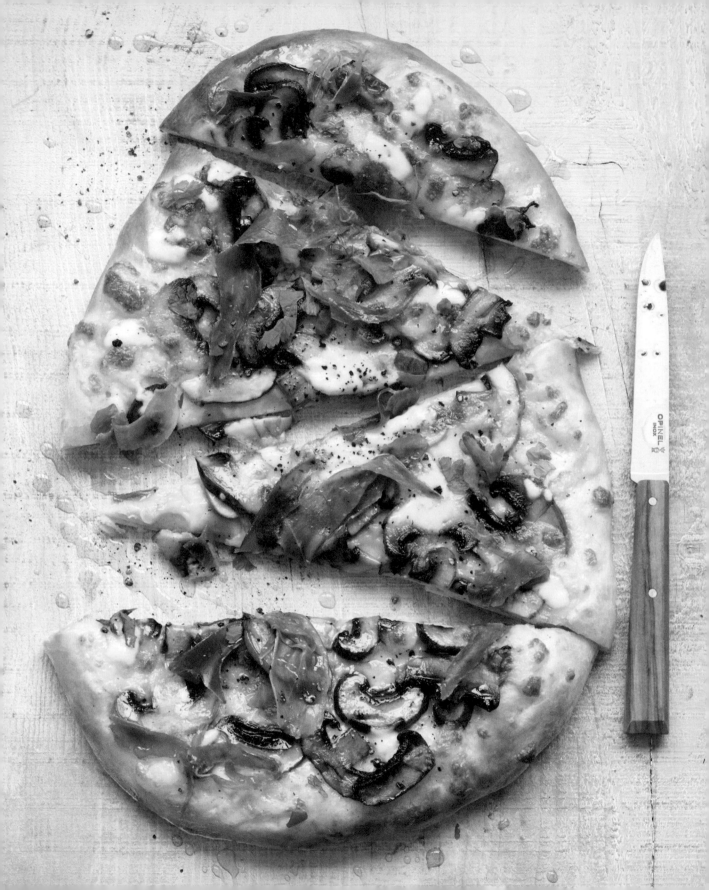

TRUFFLED MUSHROOM & PARMA HAM PIZZA Ⓜ

Making pizza from scratch is very satisfying. It also means that you can be creative with the toppings! The additions of Parma ham and a touch of truffle oil make for a stylish take on a mushroom pizza.

500 g/4 cups strong white/bread flour
1 teaspoon fast-action dried yeast
1 teaspoon salt
½ teaspoon sugar
250–275 ml/1–1¼ cups warm water
3½ tablespoons olive oil
500 g/1 lb 2 oz. white/cup mushrooms, sliced 5 mm/¼-inch thick
1 garlic clove, chopped
2 balls of mozzarella cheese, torn into pieces
4 slices of Parma ham/ prosciutto, roughly torn
a handful of freshly chopped flat-leaf parsley
1 teaspoon truffle oil
salt and freshly ground black pepper

SERVES 4

First, make the pizza dough. Place the flour, yeast, salt and sugar in a large bowl and mix together. Gradually mix in the warm water to form a soft, sticky dough. Knead the dough on a floured surface for 10 minutes, until smooth and supple.

Place the dough in a floured bowl, cover with a clean kitchen cloth or cling film/plastic wrap. Set aside in a warm place for 1 hour to rise, until the dough has doubled in size.

Preheat the oven to 250°C (475°F) Gas 9. Place 2 baking sheets in the oven to heat.

Heat a large, heavy frying pan/skillet. Add 1 tablespoon of the olive oil, heat through, then add the mushrooms. Fry over a high heat for 8 minutes, stirring now and then, until any liquid from the mushrooms has evaporated and they are lightly browned.

Add a further ½ tablespoon olive oil and heat through. Add the garlic to the oil and fry, stirring, for 1 minute. Season with salt and pepper. Set aside.

Divide the risen dough into 4 equal-sized portions. Roll out each portion on a lightly floured, clean work surface, to form a circular pizza base. Brush each pizza base evenly with ½ tablespoon of the olive oil. Sprinkle each with the fried mushrooms, dividing them evenly among the 4 bases. Dot with mozzarella pieces.

Transfer to the baking sheets, then bake in batches if necessary, in the preheated oven for 10 minutes until the dough is golden-brown.

Top the pizzas with Parma ham/prosciutto and sprinkle with parsley. Drizzle ¼ tablespoon truffle oil over each pizza, if using. Serve at once.

VE MUSHROOM, ARTICHOKE, OLIVE & CAPER PIZZA Prepare the dough and mushrooms as main recipe. Omit the Parma ham and replace with 4 chargrilled and marinated artichoke hearts, 6 pitted and halved black olives and 1 tablespoon capers. Replace the mozzarella with a handful of vegan mozzarella-style cheese (optional). Add a handful of shredded basil to the finished pizza and drizzle with extra-virgin oil, in place of the truffle oil.

LENTIL MOUSSAKA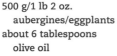

500 g/1 lb 2 oz.
aubergines/eggplants
about 6 tablespoons
olive oil
1 onion, finely chopped
1 leek, trimmed and
chopped
3 garlic cloves, chopped
1 carrot, peeled and
finely diced
6 tomatoes (about
750 g/1 lb 10 oz.),
peeled and chopped
4 tablespoons tomato
purée/paste
½ teaspoon ground
cinnamon
1 tablespoon dried oregano
2 fresh or dried bay leaves
1 teaspoon caster/
granulated sugar
200 g/1 cup dried Puy/
French green lentils
200 g/2 cups grated
vegetarian Pecorino-style
cheese
salt and freshly ground
black pepper

TOPPING
3 eggs, beaten
30 g/¼ cup plain/
all-purpose flour
500 ml/2¼ cups natural/
plain thick Greek yogurt
a pinch of freshly grated
nutmeg
salt and freshly ground
black pepper

*a 28 x 18-cm/11 x 7-inch
ovenproof dish,
generously buttered*

SERVES 6

This is a vegetarian version of a retro dish that normally includes minced/ground beef or lamb. It makes a good supper dish, served with a crisp green salad and some good bread.

Preheat the oven to 180°C (350°F) Gas 4.

Cut the aubergines/eggplants into 1-cm/³⁄₈-inch slices, and brush the cut sides with olive oil. Heat a baking sheet with sides in the oven for 5 minutes, then bake the aubergine/eggplant slices, sprinkled with a little salt, for about 30 minutes, until beginning to brown. Halfway through cooking, turn them over with a spatula, so they cook evenly.

Meanwhile, heat 3 tablespoons of the olive oil in a frying pan/skillet and fry the onion, leek and garlic over a gentle heat until soft and golden. Add the diced carrot, chopped tomatoes, tomato purée/paste, cinnamon, oregano and bay leaves, cover and simmer together for another 30 minutes or so. Stir in the sugar.

While the tomato sauce is cooking, rinse and drain the lentils, then place in a saucepan covered with cold water. Bring to the boil and simmer for about 20 minutes, until soft (bear in mind that they will not cook any further once mixed with the tomato sauce.) Drain the lentils and add to the tomato sauce, then season with salt and pepper.

Spread half of the aubergine/eggplant slices in the bottom of the prepared ovenproof dish. Cover with half of the tomato and lentil mixture, then repeat with another layer of each. Sprinkle half of the grated cheese over the surface.

To make the topping, whisk the eggs with the flour, then gently stir in the yogurt, 1 level teaspoon salt and some pepper and the grated nutmeg. Spoon this mixture over the dish of vegetables, finishing by sprinkling the remaining grated cheese over the surface.

Bake in the preheated oven for 30–40 minutes, until the top is bubbling and brown. Serve hot.

VE LENTIL & AUBERGINE BAKE WITH OLIVE OIL MASH Make the filling as main recipe but omit the grated Pecorino and the topping. Peel 800 g/1 lb 12 oz. floury potatoes and cut them into chunks. Cover with salted water in a large saucepan and add 2 peeled garlic cloves. Boil until tender, drain and mash with 2 tablespoons good olive oil. Season generously with salt and freshly ground black pepper. Spoon over the dish of filling, level the surface and bake as main recipe. Sprinkle with freshly chopped flat-leaf parsley to serve.

AUBERGINE LASAGNE

This is a great vegetarian take on a much-loved classic pasta dish, this is delicious home-cooked food with that magical Italian touch.

AUBERGINE FILLING
5 tablespoons olive oil
1 onion, chopped
1 garlic clove, chopped
1 kg/2 lb 4 oz. ripe
  tomatoes, scalded,
  skinned and chopped
  (reserve any juices),
  see page 105
handful of fresh basil
  leaves, roughly chopped
2 aubergines/eggplants,
  finely diced
about 12 lasagne sheets,
  cooked according to the
  package instructions
25 g/⅓ cup freshly grated
  vegetarian Parmesan
  cheese
salt and freshly ground
  black pepper

WHITE SAUCE
25 g/2 tablespoons butter
25 g/3½ tablespoons
  plain/all-purpose flour
300 ml/1¼ cups milk
pinch of freshly grated
  nutmeg

a 28 x 18-cm/11 x 7-inch
  ovenproof dish,
  generously oiled

SERVES 4

Heat 1 tablespoon of the oil in a large, heavy-bottomed frying pan/ skillet over a low heat. Fry the onion and garlic until softened. Add the chopped tomatoes with their juices. Season with salt and pepper.

Increase the heat, cover and bring the mixture to the boil. Uncover and cook for a further 5 minutes, stirring often, until reduced and thickened. Stir in the basil.

Heat 2 tablespoons of the oil in a separate large, heavy-bottomed frying pan/skillet set over a medium heat. Add half of the diced aubergine/ eggplant and fry, stirring often, until softened and lightly browned, then set aside. Repeat the process with the remaining oil and aubergine/ eggplant. Mix the fried aubergine/eggplant into the tomato sauce.

Preheat the oven to 200°C (400°F) Gas 6.

Make the white sauce by melting the butter in a heavy-bottomed saucepan or pot set over a low–medium heat. Stir in the flour and cook, stirring, for 1–2 minutes. Gradually pour in the milk, stirring continuously to combine. Bring the mixture to the boil and simmer until thickened. Season with salt, pepper and nutmeg.

Arrange a layer of cooked lasagne sheets in the prepared ovenproof dish. Put a layer of the aubergine/eggplant mixture over the top, then sprinkle over a little vegetarian Parmesan cheese. Repeat the process, finishing with a layer of lasagne sheets. Spread the white sauce evenly over the top, then sprinkle over the remaining vegetarian Parmesan.

Bake in the preheated oven for 40–50 minutes until golden-brown. Remove from the oven and serve at once.

M **BEEF LASAGNE** Omit the Aubergine Filling. Heat 1 tablespoon olive oil in a large saucepan over a low heat. Add 1 finely chopped onion and sauté for 10 minutes, or until soft. Turn up the heat and add 2 crushed garlic cloves and 400 g/14 oz. lean beef mince. Fry for 5 minutes, stirring frequently. Add 200 g/7 oz. roughly chopped mushrooms and cook for 5 minutes. Add a 400-g/14-oz. can of tomatoes, 1 tablespoon tomato purée/paste, 1 tablespoon dried mixed herbs and a few dashes of Worcestershire sauce. Season, bring to the boil, simmer for 15 minutes, stirring occasionally. Remove from the heat. Substitute this mixture for the Aubergine Filling as you prepare and cook the lasagne following the main recipe.

FENNEL & ROAST TOMATO LASAGNE ⓥ

A delicious and sophisticated vegetarian twist on an Italian classic.
Serve with sweet potato chips/fries for a satisfying meal.

3 fennel bulbs, thinly sliced
800 g/1 lb 12 oz. tomatoes
   on the vine
2 tablespoons olive oil
2 tablespoons balsamic
   vinegar
300 ml/1¼ cups
   double/heavy cream
100 g/1⅓ cups grated
   vegetarian Parmesan
   cheese
about 12 lasagne sheets,
   cooked according to the
   package instructions
salt and freshly ground
   black pepper

*a 28 x 18-cm/11 x 7-inch
   ovenproof dish,
   generously oiled*

SERVES 4

Preheat the oven to 180°C (350°F) Gas 4.

Spread the sliced fennel out on a roasting pan, drizzle with olive oil and sprinkle with a pinch of salt and pepper.

Put the tomatoes (still on the vine) on a separate baking sheet, drizzle with the olive oil and balsamic vinegar and season with a pinch of salt and a little freshly ground black pepper.

Put both sheets in the preheated oven and cook for 30 minutes.

Remove the fennel, pour over the cream, mix with the fennel, and return to the oven for a further 10 minutes.

Transfer the tomatoes to a large mixing bowl. Carefully remove the vine and lightly crush the tomatoes with the back of a fork. Leave the oven on.

Add most of the cheese to the fennel and cream mixture and stir, making a thick cheesy sauce with a custard-like consistency.

In the prepared ovenproof dish, start to assemble the lasagne with a thin layer of tomatoes, then a layer of lasagne sheets, followed by a layer of fennel and another layer of lasagne sheets. Continue with this pattern of layers; tomatoes, pasta, fennel, pasta, finishing with fennel, onto which you can sprinkle the remaining cheese. Cover with foil and set aside.

Remove the foil from the lasagne for the last 10 minutes of cooking to allow the top to brown.

Remove from the oven and serve.

PE SALMON & FENNEL LASAGNE To turn this into a luxurious fish dish take 2 fillets (about 170 g/6 oz.) of hot smoked salmon. Break the flesh into chunks and place them in between the tomatoes when adding this layer. (As the salmon is pre-cooked you don't need to adjust the cooking time.) If you find you have a few leftover roasted tomatoes, simply purée them in a blender, season and serve on the side as a spooning sauce.

OVEN-ROASTED ROOTS

This dish may take a little bit of preparation but the end result is a beautiful plate of food with each vegetable cooked to its full, delicious potential.

4 carrots, unpeeled
1 star anise
4 large potatoes, peeled
    and cut in half
4 parsnips, peeled and cut
    into quarters lengthways
pinch of cumin seeds
drizzle of maple syrup
1 celeriac/celery root,
    peeled and diced into
    1-cm/³⁄₈-inch cubes
1 small pumpkin, unpeeled
    and sliced into 2-cm/
    ³⁄₄-inch wedges
1 large sweet potato, peeled
    and sliced into 2-cm/
    ³⁄₄-inch rounds
1 teaspoon miso paste
2 onions, trimmed
    and quartered
a handful of fresh
    marjoram, thyme
    and sage leaves
salt and ground
    white pepper
vegetable oil, to coat

SERVES 4

Preheat the oven to 180°C (350°F) Gas 4.

Scrub the carrots with a wire scourer to clean off all the dirt and make them rough. Put in a saucepan of cold salted water and add the star anise. Set over a medium heat and bring to a low simmer for 10 minutes, then remove from the water using a slotted spoon and leave to cool. Slice in half lengthways, rub with a little vegetable oil and place on a sheet pan with a light covering of salt to season, leaving room for all the other vegetables.

Put the potatoes in a saucepan of cold salted water. Set over a medium heat and bring to a low simmer for about 15 minutes until they are just starting to flake and break up. Drain the potatoes using a fine mesh sieve/ strainer and set over the warm pan (no longer on the heat) for 10 minutes to dry out completely. Toss with a little oil and add a pinch of salt and white pepper while they are still warm. Transfer to the sheet pan with the carrots.

Rub a little vegetable oil over the parsnips and then a little maple syrup to form a thin glaze. Put on the sheet pan and sprinkle with a little salt to season. Toss the celeriac/celery root cubes with some vegetable oil and ½ teaspoon of salt and transfer to the sheet pan.

Remove any seeds from the pumpkin slices, rub with vegetable oil to coat, then sprinkle lightly with cumin seeds. Transfer to the sheet pan and arrange skin-side down. Rub the sweet potato slices with vegetable oil, then rub the flesh with the miso paste. Transfer to the sheet pan. Add the onion and drizzle with a little vegetable oil.

Sprinkle a few marjoram, sage and thyme leaves over the top and cook in the preheated oven for 30–40 minutes or until the potatoes are golden brown. Remove from the oven and serve.

Ⓜ SAUSAGE & ROOT VEGETABLE SHEET PAN Take 8 good-quality pork sausages. (If they have been seasoned with sage and seem quite herby, reduce the quantity of fresh herbs listed in the main recipe.) Add the sausages to the hot baking sheet 10 minutes into the roasting time. Simply toss them in a little oil and dot them in between the vegetables. Remove a sausage from the baking sheet and cut it through the middle to test that it is hot and cooked through before serving.

MEXICAN TORTILLA WRAPS
WITH CHIPOTLE DRESSING

2 red and 2 orange (bell) peppers, deseeded and cut into strips

3 tablespoons olive oil

2 corn on the cob/ ears of corn

400-g/14-oz. can black-eyed beans

2 ripe avocados, peeled and pitted

freshly squeezed juice of 1 lime

1 fresh red chilli/chile, deseeded and finely chopped

4 flour tortillas

large bunch of spring onions/scallions, sliced

small bunch of coriander/cilantro

sea salt and freshly ground black pepper

Vegan Cream, to serve (see page 8)

CHIPOTLE DRESSING

2 tablespoons chipotle paste

2 tablespoons olive oil

1 tablespoon red wine vinegar

2 teaspoons sugar

SERVES 4

Roasted peppers morph into the juiciest, sweetest delights and make a fantastic filling for these moreish tortilla wraps, especially when partnered with crunchy fresh corn, black-eyed beans and ripe avocado.

Preheat the oven to 190°C (375°F) Gas 5.

Scatter the (bell) peppers over a sheet pan, drizzle over the oil and roast for 15 minutes, until they are starting to soften and char.

Cut the kernels from the sweetcorn/corn cobs, add them to the pan with the pepper strips and cook for a further 10 minutes. Drain and rinse the beans, and add them to the pan to warm through for 4–5 minutes.

Meanwhile, mash the avocado flesh in a bowl and add the lime juice and chopped chilli/chile. Season to taste.

For the dressing, whisk the chipotle paste, oil, vinegar and sugar together and season to taste with salt and freshly ground black pepper.

Spread each of the tortillas with some of the avocado spread and pile with some of the bean mixture. Drizzle over some of the dressing, and scatter with a few chopped spring onions/scallions and some coriander/cilantro leaves. Roll up and serve with Vegan Cream (or regular sour cream for a vegetarian option).

M CHICKEN & BLACK BEAN WRAPS Prepare 2 chicken breasts following the Chicken & Tofu Hotpot variation on page 73. Shred the chicken into a bowl, season with lime juice, salt and pepper and add to the wrap filling. Substitute the Vegan Cream with sour cream.

STUFFED SQUASH WITH LEEKS, BLACK LENTILS & POMEGRANATE VE

Roasting the squash in its skin gives the whole vegetable such a fabulous texture and the skin is unbelievably good to eat. Serve with a rocket/arugula salad.

2 small butternut squash, halved and deseeded
4–5 tablespoons olive oil
handful of fresh thyme leaves
2 tablespoons freshly chopped rosemary
2 large leeks, trimmed and chopped
300 g/10½ oz. baby plum tomatoes
400-g/14-oz. can black beluga lentils
salt flakes and freshly ground black pepper

POMEGRANATE DRESSING
50 ml/3½ tablespoons olive oil
50 ml/3½ tablespoons pomegranate molasses

TO SERVE
50 g/scant ½ cup toasted pine nuts
3–4 tablespoons pomegranate seeds
rocket/arugula leaves

SERVES 4

Preheat the oven to 190°C (375°F) Gas 5.

Lightly score a diamond pattern into the flesh of the squash using a sharp knife. Drizzle with a little of the oil, sprinkle with the thyme and rosemary, place on a flat sheet pan and bake for 15 minutes. Remove the sheet pan from the oven and push the squash over to one side. Scatter the chopped leeks and whole baby plum tomatoes on the other side of the pan and drizzle with the remaining oil. Season with salt flakes and black pepper and return to the oven for a further 20 minutes, until the flesh of the squash is soft and the leeks and tomatoes are lightly charred.

Scoop the leeks and tomatoes into a large bowl. Drain and rinse the lentils, and add them to this bowl. Mix the olive oil and pomegranate molasses together and add about half to the lentil mixture. Pile the mixture into the squash hollows and return the sheet pan to the oven. Bake for 5 minutes, until the lentil filling is just heated through.

Remove from the oven, drizzle over the remaining pomegranate dressing, scatter with pine nuts and pomegranate seeds and add a good grinding of black pepper before serving.

V ROAST BUTTERNUT WITH BLACK LENTILS & GOAT'S CHEESE
Cut 200 g/7 oz. firm goat's cheese into pieces and fold into the lentil filling. Use this to stuff the squash and bake as main recipe. Sprinkle with extra goat's cheese along with the toasted pine nuts and drizzle with extra Pomegranate Dressing before serving.

MUSHROOM TOAD-IN-THE HOLE
WITH ONION GRAVY

Here is a vegetarian version of this classic family dish. This recipe is lighter to eat but the onion gravy makes it a satisfying and warming meal.

100 g/¾ cup plain/
    all-purpose flour
2 eggs
60 ml/¼ cup ice-cold water
100 ml/⅓ cup whole milk
6 Portobello mushrooms
salt and ground white
    pepper, to season
vegetable oil, to drizzle

GRAVY
4 onions, thinly sliced
50 g/3½ tablespoons butter
50 g/3½ tablespoons
    plain/all-purpose flour
200 ml/1 scant cup whole
    milk

*a 25 x 30-cm/10 x 12-inch
    baking dish or 4 mini
    baking dishes, lined
    with baking parchment*

SERVES 4

To make the gravy, put the onions in a heavy-based saucepan with the butter and a generous pinch of salt and cook over a low heat for 25–30 minutes, until they are just starting to turn a golden colour. Cover the onions with the flour and continue to cook, turning the onions constantly for a further 5 minutes. With the onions still on the heat, slowly add the milk, stirring the mixture until all of the milk has been combined into a thick gravy. Add some water if needed, to achieve the desired viscosity.

To make the batter, add the flour and a pinch of salt and pepper to a bowl. Make a well in the middle of the flour and break both eggs into it. Using a whisk, mix the eggs and flour together, starting slowly from the centre. Once the ingredients are mixed, gradually add the water, mixing to a thick paste. Finally, add the milk, whilst continually mixing with the whisk until the batter is smooth. Cover and chill in the fridge for 20 minutes.

Preheat the oven to 180°C (350°F) Gas 4.

Drizzle the mushrooms with oil and sprinkle with a dusting of salt and pepper. Place them, gill-side up, in the baking dish or dishes and bake in the preheated oven for 15–20 minutes, until they are just starting to turn golden.

Remove from the oven and turn the oven up to 200°C (400°F) Gas 6. Pour the batter over the mushrooms and return to the oven for a further 15–20 minutes, until the batter has risen and is golden brown and crispy on top.

Remove the toad-in-the-hole from the baking dish or dishes and take off the baking parchment. If whole, slice into four pieces and serve hot with lashings of onion gravy.

M **SAUSAGE TOAD-IN-THE-HOLE** Omit the mushrooms. Prepare the batter as main recipe. Take 8 plain pork sausages and put them in the roasting pan. Add 1 tablespoon sunflower oil, toss the sausages in it to coat, then roast for 15 minutes in an oven preheated to 200°C (400°F) Gas 6. Take the hot pan from the oven and quickly pour in the batter, then bake for about 40 minutes, or until the batter is cooked through, well risen and crisp.

HARISSA-BAKED SQUASH
WITH AVOCADO & EGGS

The addition of spicy harissa to the already colourful flavour and texture combination of green avocado, bright orange butternut squash and eggs, is the ideal way to marry all of these ingredients together. It's rich and tangy in flavour, but the mellowness of the other ingredients contrasts well.

2 tablespoons harissa paste
2 tablespoons olive oil
550 g/1 lb 3 oz. butternut
squash, peeled, deseeded
and roughly chopped into
2-cm/³⁄₄-inch cubes
1 ripe avocado, peeled,
stoned/pitted and
thinly sliced
freshly squeezed juice
of 1 lemon
60 g/½ cup stoned/pitted
black olives
15 cherry tomatoes
4 eggs
freshly ground
black pepper

SERVES 2

Preheat the oven to 200°C (400°F) Gas 6.

Stir together the harissa paste and olive oil in a large bowl then toss in the butternut squash and stir again to coat the squash.

Put the butternut squash on a sheet pan with sides and bake in the preheated oven for 30 minutes.

Meanwhile, prepare the avocado and squeeze over the lemon juice to prevent it from turning brown. After 30 minutes, add the olives, tomatoes and avocado to the butternut squash and bake for a further 10 minutes.

Make four wells in the vegetables and crack in the eggs. Bake for another 6–9 minutes until the egg whites are cooked. Season with freshly ground black pepper and serve immediately

M **BREAKFAST SHEET PAN WITH CHORIZO & EGGS** Omit the olives and add a 200–250-g/7–8 oz. package (about 10–12) of Spanish mini cooking chorizo. Add these to the baking sheet with the tomatoes and avocado. (If the chorizo you are using is particularly spicy, reduce the amount of harissa paste in the main recipe to 1 tablespoon.) Finish as main recipe.

ROAST CAULIFLOWER SALAD
WITH TURMERIC DRESSING VE

1 large cauliflower
6 tablespoons olive oil
1 tablespoon ground
    coriander
1 tablespoon ground cumin
1 tablespoon fennel seeds
1 teaspoon dried chilli/
    red pepper flakes
1 tablespoon demerara/
    turbinado sugar
2 red (bell) peppers,
    deseeded and cut
    into strips
3 red onions, cut into
    wedges
200 g/7 oz. cherry tomatoes,
    halved
400-g/14-oz. can black
    beluga lentils, drained
    and rinsed
2–3 tablespoons sultanas/
    golden raisins
1 small, ripe mango, peeled,
    stoned/pitted and diced
bunch of fresh coriander/
    cilantro, roughly chopped
salt and freshly ground
    black pepper

TURMERIC DRESSING
25 g/1 oz. fresh turmeric,
    peeled and finely grated
2-cm/3/4-inch piece of fresh
    ginger, peeled and grated
2 garlic cloves, finely grated
2 tablespoons tahini paste
zest and juice of 1 lime
4 tablespoons olive oil
1 teaspoon caster/
    granulated sugar
1–2 tablespoons maple
    syrup

SERVES 4

The fresh turmeric dressing takes this dish to another level. Neon-orange turmeric root has a more zippy flavour than dried turmeric. Its increasing popularity means that it is now fairly readily available.

Preheat the oven to 190°C (375°F) Gas 5.

Break the cauliflower into florets. Pour the oil into a large bowl, and add the coriander, cumin, fennel seeds, chilli/red pepper flakes and sugar. Give everything a good stir, season with salt and pepper, and toss the cauliflower florets into the mixture to coat. Spread them over a large sheet pan. Scatter the red (bell) peppers, onion wedges and cherry tomatoes over the sheet pan and mix. Roast for 20–25 minutes (give everything a stir halfway through the cooking time), until the cauliflower is cooked but still has some bite.

Stir the lentils gently into the roasted vegetables. Return the sheet pan to the oven for 5 minutes, until the lentils are just heated through. Remove the pan from the oven and scatter over the sultanas/raisins. Scatter the mango over the salad and garnish with the coriander/cilantro.

For the dressing, put the grated turmeric and ginger into a bowl. Add all the remaining ingredients and 3½ tablespoons water and whisk together until smooth. Season to taste, drizzle over the salad and serve.

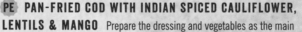

PE **PAN-FRIED COD WITH INDIAN SPICED CAULIFLOWER, LENTILS & MANGO** Prepare the dressing and vegetables as the main recipe, omitting the sultanas/golden raisins. Take 4 x 140-g/5-oz. skinless cod fillets. Add 1 tablespoon each of olive oil and butter to a large frying pan/skillet set over a medium-high heat. Lightly dust each cod fillet with seasoned plain/all-purpose flour and add to the pan. Fry the fish for 2–3 minutes on each side until lightly golden. Serve on top of the cauliflower salad, with the Turmeric Dressing drizzled over the top.

ROASTED HERITAGE BEETROOTS WITH GREEN LENTILS & BALSAMIC DRESSING VE

This is a pretty special dish for anyone following a plant-based diet. The beetroots/beets are both beautiful to look at and delicious to eat!

1 kg/2 lb 4 oz. mixed heritage beetroots/beets
3 red onions, cut into wedges
250 g/3½ cups sliced chestnut/cremini mushrooms
3 tablespoons olive oil
5–6 fresh rosemary sprigs, chopped
400-g/14-oz. can green lentils
freshly chopped mixed green herbs (dill, chives, parsley), to serve

BALSAMIC DRESSING
6 tablespoons olive oil
3 tablespoons good-quality balsamic vinegar
1 teaspoon caster/granulated sugar
1 garlic clove, finely grated

SERVES 4

Preheat the oven to 190°C (375°F) Gas 5.

Peel the beetroots/beets and cut them into wedges. Arrange them over the base of a sheet pan. Add the onions to the pan and scatter the mushrooms evenly over the top. Drizzle with olive oil and scatter over the chopped rosemary. Roast for about 45–50 minutes, until the beetroots/beets are soft.

Drain and rinse the lentils and spoon them onto the sheet pan. Return the pan to the oven for 5 minutes, until the lentils are heated through.

Mix the olive oil, balsamic vinegar, sugar and garlic together. Remove the pan from the oven, drizzle over the dressing, scatter over the freshly chopped herbs and serve warm, or at room temperature.

_____ _____ _____ _____ _____

V ROASTED BEETROOT WITH PUY LENTILS, BLUE CHEESE & BALSAMIC DRESSING Roast the beetroot/beets as main recipe. Substitute Puy lentils for green lentils and add 200 g/7 oz. firm vegetarian blue cheese (like Roquefort or Gorgonzola in style). Cut it into cubes and scatter pieces over the finished dish whilst still warm so it turns molten with the heat.

_____ _____ _____ _____ _____

INDEX

CREDITS

RECIPE CREDITS

All flexitarian variations
devised by Julia Charles.

**Chloe Coker & Jane
Montgomery**
Beetroot risotto
Winter vegetable stew with
herbed dumplings

Ross Dobson
Gnocchetti with smokey chorizo
& seared prawns/shrimp
Smoked trout fattoush with
sumac
Tenderstem broccoli, shiitake
& tofu omelette

Amy Ruth Finegold
Soba noodle bowl with pak choi,
cashews & tamari sauce
Spicy crab sauce with quinoa
spaghetti

Mat Follas
Asparagus risotto
Charred Caesar salad with
garlic croutons
Fennel & roast tomato lasagne
Fennel, watercress, red onion
& thyme gratin
Miso-roasted roots
Mushroom toad-in-the whole
with onion gravy
Thai-style vegetables en
papillote with noodles
Tomato tacos with guacamole
Vegan cheese
Vegan cream
Vegetable jambalaya

Liz Franklin
Baked oat milk porridge with
pears, almonds & date syrup

Mexican tortilla wraps with
chipotle dressing
Roast cauliflower salad with
turmeric dressing
Roasted heritage beetroot[s]
with green lentils & balsamic
dressing
Salt-baked beetroot & mango
with nerigoma dressing
Stuffed squash with leeks,
black lentils & pomegranate

Dunja Gulin
Breakfast muffins
Creamy avocado sauce with
spelt spaghetti
Tofu scramble
Velvety pumpkin & red lentil
soup

Vicky Jones
Beans a la Bourguignonne with
garlic & parsley butter
Borlotti bean & fennel stew
Catalan rice with smoked
haddock & roasted peppers
Cheesy lentil bake
Lentil moussaka
Oven-baked Greek butter beans
in tomato sauce
Salad of flageolet beans &
fennel
Syrian aubergine & chickpea
ragout with yogurt garlic
sauce

Jenny Linford
Aubergine lasagne
Chickpea & mushroom freekeh
pilaf
Eggs en cocotte with
mushrooms
Halloumi & vegetable kebabs
with bay leaves
Hazelnut, mushroom & bulgur

wheat salad
Kachumber salad
Mac 'n' cheese with mushrooms
& ham
Melon, tomato & feta salad
Mushroom & bean chili sin
carne
Mushroom burgers
Mushroom, cannellini bean
& tuna salad
Pesto-stuffed mushrooms
Puy lentil & squash casserole
with quinoa
Spiced almond pilaf
Stuffed mushrooms
Tabbouleh
Tofu & mushroom hot pot
Truffled mushroom & Parma
ham pizza
Tunisian eggs

Louise Pickford
Cauliflower-stuffed pacos
with tahini & lime yogurt
Pink pancakes with goat's
cheese, onion relish &
walnuts
Seeded baked pancake with
berries & raw cocoa sauce

Jenny Tschiesche
Butternut & Cauliflower lentil
korma
Grain-free granola
Harissa-baked squash with
avocado & eggs

Leah Vanderveldt
Chickpea socca pancakes with
mushrooms & thyme

Belinda Williams
Creamy celeriac & white bean
soup with hazelnuts
Vegetable minestrone

PHOTOGRAPHY CREDITS

Jan Baldwin 43

Simon Brown 5

Peter Cassidy 2, 22, 49, 61, 62,
104, 124

Richard Jung 41

Mowie Kay 15, 26

Alex Luck 39

Steve Painter 6, 9bl, 10, 14, 17,
30–33, 42, 46, 57, 64–68, 99, 105,
108, 111–115, 127, 128, 131-140

William Reavell 13, 18–20, 48,
71, 75–79, 83, 85-87, 92, 103, 106,
107, 117–119, 123, 130

Christopher Scholey 110

Ian Wallace 25, 34–37

Kate Whitaker 1, 54, 96

Clare Winfield 4, 9al, ar & br, 21,
29, 38, 45, 50–53, 58–60, 72, 80,
84, 88–91, 95, 100, 101, 116, 120,
141

All Illustrations by
Harriet Popham
www.harrietpopham.com